CAMBRIDGE LIBRARY COLLECTION

Books of enduring scholarly value

Polar Exploration

This series includes accounts, by eye-witnesses and contemporaries, of early expeditions to the Arctic and the Antarctic. Huge resources were invested in such endeavours, particularly the search for the North-West Passage, which, if successful, promised enormous strategic and commercial rewards. Cartographers and scientists travelled with many of the expeditions, and their work made important contributions to earth sciences, climatology, botany and zoology. They also brought back anthropological information about the indigenous peoples of the Arctic region and the southern fringes of the American continent. The series further includes dramatic and poignant accounts of the harsh realities of working in extreme conditions and utter isolation in bygone centuries.

The Franklin Expedition from First to Last

Having participated in a rescue mission to aid John Ross in the Arctic in the 1830s, traveller and surgeon Richard King (1810/11–76) considered himself qualified to suggest where the missing expedition of Sir John Franklin, which had set off in 1845, could be found. In his letters to periodicals, government ministers and the Admiralty, published in this collection in 1855, King argues that the missing party would be located near the mouth of the Great Fish River. He volunteered to lead a search expedition, but was ignored. By 1859, remains of the Franklin party had been discovered near to where King said they would be. These letters tell the story of his campaign, throwing light on an interesting chapter in the history of polar exploration and the understanding of the Canadian Arctic. Several other works on Franklin's last expedition and the subsequent searches are also reissued in this series.

Cambridge University Press has long been a pioneer in the reissuing of out-of-print titles from its own backlist, producing digital reprints of books that are still sought after by scholars and students but could not be reprinted economically using traditional technology. The Cambridge Library Collection extends this activity to a wider range of books which are still of importance to researchers and professionals, either for the source material they contain, or as landmarks in the history of their academic discipline.

Drawing from the world-renowned collections in the Cambridge University Library and other partner libraries, and guided by the advice of experts in each subject area, Cambridge University Press is using state-of-the-art scanning machines in its own Printing House to capture the content of each book selected for inclusion. The files are processed to give a consistently clear, crisp image, and the books finished to the high quality standard for which the Press is recognised around the world. The latest print-on-demand technology ensures that the books will remain available indefinitely, and that orders for single or multiple copies can quickly be supplied.

The Cambridge Library Collection brings back to life books of enduring scholarly value (including out-of-copyright works originally issued by other publishers) across a wide range of disciplines in the humanities and social sciences and in science and technology.

The Franklin Expedition from First to Last

Richard King

Cambridge University Press

CAMBRIDGE
UNIVERSITY PRESS

University Printing House, Cambridge, CB2 8BS, United Kingdom

Published in the United States of America by Cambridge University Press, New York

www.cambridge.org
Information on this title: www.cambridge.org/9781108071642

This edition first published 1855
This digitally printed version 2014

ISBN 978-1-108-07164-2 Paperback

KING ISLAND FROM KING CACHE OF MONTREAL ISLAND; POINT OGLE IN THE DISTANCE.
DEATH SPOT OF THE FRANKLIN EXPEDITION.

THE FRANKLIN EXPEDITION

FROM

FIRST TO LAST.

BY

D[R] KING, MD.

LONDON.
JOHN CHURCHILL, NEW BURLINGTON STREET.
1855.

PREFACE.

A letter of thanks for a *past* search by the Great Fish River for Sir John Ross, and an earnest appeal for a *future* search by the Great Fish River for Sir John Franklin, is an introduction due to myself and to the press. Had the *past*, as an earnest of the *future*, been accepted—had the *appeal* in behalf of a tried servant on the one hand, and of suffering humanity on the other, been heard, The Franklin Expedition, humanly speaking, would now be alive, occupied in the great effort against a powerful enemy.

The Times, 13th October, '35.

" (Advertisement.)

" To the Subscribers to the Land Journey in search of Sir John Ross.

" It is most gratifying to the committee

"to be enabled to state, that almost without "exception, the most unqualified meed of "approbation seems due to the exertions "of every one concerned. In an especial "manner, however, is this testimony due "to Sir George Back himself, to Dr. King, "his physician, and only accompanying "officer, and to eight brave men—James "McKay, George Sinclair, Peter Taylor[1], "John Ross[2], Charles Mackenzie, James "Spence, William Malley, and Hugh "Carron—who proceeded with their gallant "officers in a single boat to the Polar Sea. "The dangers, difficulties, and hardships "to which they were thus exposed were "greatly beyond what had been anticipated; "but not, as it proved, beyond their power "to surmount.

"To all concerned, then, the committee "takes the liberty of now tendering its "warmest thanks. These, perhaps, ought "to be first addressed to the subscribers, "without whose prompt and generous

[1] These three gallant fellows accompanied Mr. T. Simpson in his memorable journey.

[2] Now one of Her Majesty's Yeomen of the Guard.

" liberality the scheme must have fallen to
" the ground when first proposed. They
" are afterwards, however, especially due to
" Sir George Back, Dr. King, and those
" actually employed in the expedition; and
" they are also respectfully tendered to all
" co-operators with it; in particular to the
" governor, deputy-governor, and directors
" of the Hudson Bay Company; to the
" generous citizens of the United States;
" to his Excellency Lord Aylmer, Governor-
" General of the two Canadas; and others
" who promoted its objects in Montreal.

" WILLIAM BOWLES,

" *Chairman.*

" 21, *Regent Street, Oct.* 9."

The *Athenæum*, 13th November, '47.

" The silence which has enveloped the
" proceedings of Sir John Franklin and his
" gallant party of Northern explorers having
" extended now beyond all limits consistent
" with a confidence in their security, the
" anxiety of the Admiralty is awakened in
" their behalf; and if a few days more shall
" pass without tidings of their whereabout,

" a party will be dispatched to seek them
" out, or come upon the traces of their fate.
" Coincidently with this renewal of the
" fears which have followed these sea ex-
" peditions for the solution of the polar
" problem comes the intelligence of the
" complete success of a land journey, which
" has increased the peril of the Franklin
" attempt, and heightened the uneasiness
" as to its result. As Dr. King has for
" years been urging, through our columns
" and elsewhere, geographical views which
" the progress of discovery has now con-
" firmed,—as well as practical opinions on
" the best means by which Arctic discovery
" was to be pursued, that have been singu-
" larly justified by the series of events,—
" and as he entertains certain views as to
" the direction and methods in which a
" party seeking Sir John Franklin should
" now proceed, that have also been promul-
" gated in this paper, we feel it only due to
" him to point out that his opinions are
" entitled at the least to serious attention,
" in view of the test which they have already
" successfully stood. We have suffered Dr.

" King from time to time to argue his case " in our columns without taking any part " of our own in his argument or against it; " but it is incumbent on us now to direct " attention to the confirmation which his " views have already received from events " —and the right which that circumstance " unquestionably gives him to a hearing " wherever the measures best adapted for " the recovery of Sir John Franklin and his " band of adventurers have to be discussed.

" In the narrative of his journey, pub- " lished in 1836[3], Dr. King states:—' The " ' success of the Polar land journeys has " ' very satisfactorily shewn that to such a " ' service only England will in all proba- " ' bility be indebted for the survey of the " ' coast now unexplored, and for the know- " ' ledge of any passage about Regent Inlet.' " The surveys of Mr. Thomas Simpson and " Dr. Rae are monuments to the truth of " this remark. Dr. King did not content " himself with mere vague or authoritative " assertion. The last thirty-nine pages of

[3] King's "Journey to the Arctic Ocean by the Great Fish River," Vol. ii. p. 303.

" the second volume of his narrative are " full of facts in support of his views. In a " communication on the subject, addressed " to the Geographical Society in 1836[4], he " remarks:—

" Having maturely considered the best means to be adopted for a further survey of the Northern coast of America, I have come to the following conclusions:— A party, consisting of an officer and six men, should proceed in a North-canoe—the smallest vessel in use in the country—passing from Montreal in Lower Canada, by the rivers Hudson and Uttawa, Lakes Huron, Superior, and Winnipic, to the Athabasca; and then due North, by a route well known to the Chipewyans, to a river to the Eastward of Fort Reliance called the Fish River. On its banks the party should winter; as, upon Indian authority, not far from its source a tributary to the Great Fish River takes its rise, which is said to disembogue somewhere below the Musk-Ox Rapid, and is probably Baillie River. Early in the spring the party should proceed by that stream down the Great Fish River to its mouth; and having ascended the inlet to Cape Hay, coast along until the Isthmus of Boothia be either met with or proved not to exist. If the land of North Somerset is found to be continuous with the land forming Repulse Bay, it may then be advisable to fit out a sea expedition, to try for a passage about the

[4] King's " Journey to the Arctic Ocean by the Great Fish River," vol ii. p. 301.

broken land around Melville Island. While, however, the passage by Regent Inlet remains in doubt, I consider it would be highly impolitic to send out an expedition on a large and expensive scale."

" Dr. King then proceeds to argue in " favour of a small rather than a large " number of persons to compose the ex- " ploring party.—

" The precedents in favour of a small party will be found to be many. Sir Alexander M'Kenzie made all his discoveries in a North-canoe, and Hearne discovered the mouth of the Coppermine River without even a single white attendant. Park and Lander, who succeeded when alone, failed and lost their lives when accompanied by a party; and Captain Burnes is acknowledged to have made his journey in the most judicious manner by so conducting himself that he in general made friends of those races who have invariably been hostile to all strangers. The plan which I have sketched," continues Dr. King, " was conceived and matured whilst I was in the Indian country; and the most able of my companions are anxious to aid me in carrying it into execution. The question has been asked, how I can anticipate success in an undertaking which has baffled a Franklin and a Back? I will state in reply, that if I were to pursue the plan adopted by these officers—of fixing upon a wintering ground so situated as to oblige me to drag boat and baggage over some two hundred miles of ice, to reach that stream which is to carry me to the scene of discovery, and, when there, to embark in a vessel that I knew my whole force to be incapable of managing—very far from expecting to achieve more than those officers have done, I very much question if I could effect so much.

"In selecting my wintering ground, I have not only borne in mind the appalling calamities which befel the natives at Fort Reliance, occasioned by the presence of Sir George Back's party, but the long and laborious duty of conveying boat and baggage to Musk-Ox Rapid. Neither was it likely I should forget the transport of the baggage across the Great Slave Lake, and of the boat over Portage la Loche; not merely because those undertakings were conceived and accomplished after Sir George Back had consigned the expedition to my charge, but because I believe them to have been hitherto unequalled.

"In the selection of my vessel I have taken care to provide myself with one that two men are sufficient to convey over any obstacle that the previous Expeditions have hitherto had to contend with,—one that is in use among the natives, and one in which the fur-traders, from long experience, have found to be most adequate in traversing unknown ground. It was not only the vessel in use with Sir Alexander M'Kenzie and Hearne, but it was in such a vessel Sir John Franklin surveyed the Copper Mine River, and traced the coast-line to Point Turnagain; which spot, since more unwieldy vessels have been used, has not been again reached, although two expeditions have sailed from England for that purpose, the one at an expense of about forty thousand pounds, and the other at seven thousand."

" Point Turnagain, our readers know, has " since been reached, and the land between " it and the Great Fish River Estuary " surveyed by *a small land party.*"

" By the plan I propose, time as well as manual labour will be saved; and those obstacles which have arrested the progress of former expeditions, such as falls, fissures, mountains and masses of ice, no longer present insurmountable barriers against arctic research. It is by avoiding those errors into which former commanders have fallen, and by taking advantage of suggestions dictated by experience, that I hope to effect more than my predecessors, and it is seldom that by any other course great objects can be achieved."

" The communicator of Dr. King's paper " to the Geographical Society, put the " views of the former, as to the practical " part of the questions in issue, in a few " clear paragraphs."

" The researches of our countrymen have already greatly reduced the extent of the northern coast of America respecting which doubt or ignorance exists. The investigation of this remaining portion may be undertaken either by sea or by land. When I call to mind how large a portion of the sea expeditions have been either unsuccessful, or attended with prodigious loss or risk—how great an expense they unavoidably incur compared with the amount of real advantage to be expected, it does seem well worthy the consideration of the Geographical Society, whether it be right to recommend to the Government the equipment of a fresh expedition of this kind, until one or more points have been settled by the more economical as well as the more promising agency of a land journey.

" Although a land journey towards the northern coast of North America may be regarded as less expensive and less dangerous than a sea expedition, and at the present moment more likely to obtain accessions to science and commerce, they may greatly vary amongst themselves in all these respects, according to the mode in which they may be undertaken. They may, however, be all comprised in two classes.

" To the first class belong small companies, travelling with the least possible encumbrance, and strictly adopting the mode of proceeding and the means of subsistence in use amongst the natives of the country and the traders who visit them. Individuals uniting physical ability, both for doing and suffering, necessary to meet the dangers and fatigues of this mode of travelling, with talents and acquirements necessary to render their journey availing for the purposes of science, have already effected much at a very trifling outlay. Hearne and Mackenzie prove the truth of this assertion.

" The second class consists of those expeditions which possess a more organised and systematic form, being composed of a company of men and officers accustomed to military or naval service, seldom or never amounting to a smaller number than two or three officers and eighteen or twenty men, and consequently requiring a considerable amount of baggage For the conveyance of these men and their stores the small canoes of the country, which are readily made, repaired, and transported, are quite inadequate. Boats of larger dimensions are therefore had recourse to, which are easily damaged, are with difficulty repaired, and are too cumbrous to be conveyed across the portages when the distance is great or the ground uneven. These evils are not theoretical; they have been proved by fearful experience, and have been the cause of immense difficulty or failure. Companies of the size now under consideration, though they form but a small military troop, are too large to travel with advantage through a country in which the means of subsistence are very scanty and still more precarious. The difficulties which they have to encounter are infinitely increased when the individuals comprising the company are not practically acquainted with the mode of travelling through the district to be crossed, and consequently cannot be separated from each other without the greatest danger of fatally losing their way; on which account they cannot seek game and other sources of subsistence. From want of experience they are unable either to bear the burdens or travel the distance which a Canadian or an Indian would disregard. Time, the most important element in northern expeditions, is inevitably lost, and neither the energy nor the genius of the commanding officer can retrieve the error when the season is advanced upon them.

" The expedition of which Dr. King has sketched the accompanying outline—for which he has already made many necessary preparations, and in which an adequate number of his former companions are anxious to accompany him—falls under the first or small class of land journies to which I have alluded. The expense which it would probably incur is small, compared with that of any expedition of the second class;—so small indeed, that its adequacy has been called in question. It must, however, be recollected that the expedition has to pass through a country in which money is of no avail; that, with the exception of articles to be used in barter with the Indians, the skill and experience of the leader, and the strength and prowess of his companions, are the only availing resources. In such a journey the experience and ability of the leader is the desideratum of the first importance; and it is scarcely to be measured or represented by money. This desideratum, Dr. King, the companion of Sir George Back—the joint, and, for a considerable time, the sole conductor of his company—is not only ready to offer, but he is also generously willing to bear a considerable part of the pecuniary expense."

" Dr. King's paper, we are told, was not " acknowledged either to himself or to its " communicator; nor was it read before " the Geographical Society, nor published " in its journal—though communications " on the same subject, and at the same " time, were both read and published from " Sir J. Ross, Sir J. Franklin, Sir J.

" Barrow, Sir J. Richardson, and Sir F. " Beaufort[5]. Why the Geographical Society " should have thus treated Dr. King, we " know not; but we believe it is a fact " that on the return of the expedition in " search of Sir J. Ross, Dr. King differed " materially from Sir George Back in " regard to the survey which that gallant " officer had made. He maintained that " Cape Hay was not, as Sir George Back " had drawn it, the Northern extreme of " the Western boundary of the Great Fish " River Estuary[6]—that the Polar Sea to " the North of Lake Garry formed a great " bay[7]—and that North Somerset was a " Peninsula. All these opinions have now " been established as truths. The existence " of the Great Bay North of Lake Garry, " and the continuity of the land North of " Cape Hay, were proved by Mr. Thomas

[5] " Journal of the Royal Geographical Society," vol. vi.

[6] King's " Journey to the Arctic Ocean by the Great " Fish River," vol. ii. p. 26.

[7] *Idem*, p. 77.

"Simpson in 1830[8]—and the Peninsularity
"of North Somerset is now at length
"determined by Dr. Rae.

"The verification of these important
"features entitles Dr. King, as we have
"said, to a high position as a scientific
"geographer. For instance;—the ex-
"istence of such a coast as encloses the
"Great Bay much facilitated the progress
"of Mr. Thomas Simpson; and it was
"'the probability of its existence,' to use
"Dr. King's own words, 'which induced
"'him to be so sanguine of success as to
"'volunteer to the Secretary of State for
"'the Colonies for the time being, year
"'after year, to conduct such an expedition
"'as Mr. Thomas Simpson undertook and
"'successfully carried out; for if several
"'jutting points of land had occupied the
"'space of that bay, not one season, but
"'several seasons, would have been re-
"'quired for its survey.' The discovery
"of land North of Cape Hay was even

[8] Despatch of Mr. Simpson in the *Athenæum*, No. 652.

" more important; for it was strong evi-
" dence, in support of the Esquimaux
" Chart, of North Somerset being a Pen-
" insula. Dr. King remarks in 1836[9]—
" ' From Cape Hay, the land, blue in the
" ' distance, trended North-North-East,
" ' where it dipped the horizon; but a
" ' little space, however, intervened to a
" ' land gradually rising into boldness,
" ' following a North-Westerly course, the
" ' extremes of which were named Points
" ' Ross and Booth. My impression was
" ' that the sea formed a deep bay in that
" ' direction.' By Dr. Rae's despatch, this is
" proved to be true to the very letter. It
" was his own observations, coupled with
" the fact that no current passed through
" the Fury and Hecla Strait, that led Dr.
" King to put the utmost confidence in
" the Esquimaux Chart as published by
" Sir John Ross. The Hydrographer to
" the Admiralty, Sir Francis Beaufort,
" flung aside the Esquimaux Chart and
" Dr. King's observations—and erased the
" dotted lines which made North Somerset

[9] King's "Arctic Ocean," vol. ii. p. 26.

" a Peninsula[10]. Dr. King, in a paper read
" before the British Association at York,
" and published in the 'London, Edin-
" 'burgh, and Dublin Philosophical Journal
" 'of Science,' for December 1844, says:—
" 'Considerable importance has been at-
" 'tached to the land of North Somerset,
" 'from a belief that it is an island; which,
" 'if proved, would at once solve the grand
" 'problem of three centuries—the dis-
" 'covery of the North-West passage. This
" 'is evidently an error; for if insular, its
" 'separation can be but of trifling extent
" '—otherwise there would be a strong
" 'current setting through the Fury and
" 'Hecla Strait; whereas, according to Sir
" 'Edward Parry, there is no current—
" 'while the absence of a current through
" 'that Strait is a powerful argument in
" 'favour of its being a Peninsula.'

" Further, in a letter addressed to Sir
" John Barrow, as Secretary to the Ad-
" miralty, dated Jan. 8, 1845[11], Dr. King
" says:—

[10] See Admiralty Chart of Baffin Bay.

[11] See *Athenæum*, No. 898.

"You implicitly believe North Somerset to be an island, and the Fury and Hecla Strait to be the Atlantic outlet of the Polar Sea[12]. Where are the facts? Sir Edward Parry, who discovered the Fury and Hecla Strait, and it has not been visited since his time, has distinctly stated that there is no current in the Fury and Hecla Strait. Sir John Ross has published an Esquimaux Chart of North Somerset, wherein it is shewn to be a Peninsula. That, you will say, rests upon Indian information. It does, and so did the existence of the Polar Sea, the Fury and Hecla Strait, the Isthmus of Boothia, and Melville Peninsula. And who doubts the accuracy of these Polar fishermen in these respects On the contrary, their geographical knowledge is the admiration of the world. Are you then justified in doubting them in this solitary instance? The same woman—women are the geographers at the Pole—who figured that extraordinary Isthmus, the Isthmus of Boothia, figured that land over which you are attempting to throw a doubt. When I contended for this point in 1836, you referred to Sir George Back's decided opinion[13] of the termination of the Eastern boundary of the Great Fish River Estuary at Cape Hay —in which belief the gallant commander, to do honour to the Earl of Ripon, the chief promoter of the expedition, named an island, lying off the Cape, Ripon Island. But Cape Hay has now lost its importance, and Ripon Island is not in existence; Cape Britannia

[12] Geographical Society's Journal, vol. vi. p. 35.

[13] Back's Narrative, p. 408.

occupies the place of Ripon Island, and you are thus informed by that great traveller, Simpson, whose death all deplore, that I was right, and that Sir George Back was wrong."

"Lastly, in a letter to Earl Grey, as " lately as the 10th of June last[14], Dr. King " states,—' North Somerset is a Peninsula " ' forming the North-Eastern corner of " ' America, the Western shore of Regent " ' Inlet, and the Eastern shore of the Great " ' Fish River.'

"We have thought it right, we repeat, " in justice to Dr. King, that these facts " should be known. They cannot but give " weight to the opinions which he has " explained to Earl Grey as to the probable " position of Sir John Franklin's Expe- " dition and the best means of rescuing it."

The Times, 14th June, '47.

"We understand that Dr. King, the " medical officer, and, for a considerable " period, the commanding officer of the " land journey in search of Sir John Ross, " has addressed a letter to Earl Grey,

[14] See *Athanæum, ante*, p. 621.

" volunteering his services in search of Sir " John Franklin. Dr. King maintains " that, to save The Franklin Expedition, it " would be futile to attempt to convey " provisions overland to him. He proposes, " therefore, to the Government to send out " one or more ships laden with provisions, " next Spring, to the Western Land of " North Somerset, where he maintains, for " several reasons, Sir John Franklin will " be found, and, at the same time, to call " upon the Hudson Bay Company to " store up provisions in their trading houses " on the Mackenzie River and the Great " Slave Lake. He then proposes, in " company with any officer the Govern- " ment may appoint, to be the messenger " of such news to Sir John Franklin, and, " at the same time, to take with him Indian " guides for the conveyance of the veteran " officer and his party, either to the pro- " vision stores on the Mackenzie River or " the Great Slave Lake, or to the provision " vessels at the Western Land of North " Somerset as may be most desirable. He " maintains that he is the only person who

" has all the requisites for such a journey,
" —youth, health, great physical strength,
" and an intimate acquaintance with the
" country and the Indians. He has placed
" a heavy responsibility on Earl Grey, for
" he does not hesitate to state it is the
" only plan which can afford that relief to
" Sir John Franklin which he has a right
" to expect from the Government. Sir
" John Franklin, he asserts, should not
" have sailed in face of the facts he laid
" before the late Government; for, to
" use his own words, 'it was altogether
" 'impracticable, as the expedition would
" 'have to *take the ice*, as the pushing
" 'through an ice-blocked sea is termed,
" 'in utter ignorance of the extent of its
" 'dangers, and certainly with no better
" 'prospect before it than that which befel
" 'Sir John Ross, whose escape from a
" 'perilous position of four years' duration
" 'was admitted by all to have been almost
" 'miraculous. As it now stands, there-
" 'fore, it is imperative on the Government
" 'to use every means to save the lost party
" 'from the death of starvation.'"

The *Sunday Times* copied the preceding article.

The *Pictorial Times*, 4th December, '47.

"We take considerable interest in the "search for Sir John Franklin, but, like "many others, turn with disgust from its "discussion, from the gross unfairness with "which the claims of Dr. King to be re- "cognised as the most correct authority "upon the geography of the Arctic Regions, "and the best qualified to conduct any "expedition in search of the missing ad- "venturers, are met with by the authorities "in whose hands are placed the arrange- "ments for pursuing the contemplated "search."

The *Nautical Standard*, 12th June, '47.

"The whole of Dr. King's letter to Earl "Grey so abounds in tersely stated facts, "and these facts are of a nature so im- "portant to the recovery of Sir John "Franklin, while the principles laid down "are so essential to the prosecution of all "further Arctic discovery, that we feel

" ourselves called upon to state our con-
" viction that Dr. King's plans deserve the
" immediate attention of Government. They
" are put forth by a gentleman well known
" in the annals of arctic discovery, highly
" respected in his profession, and most
" deservedly esteemed by scientific societies,
" to whose interest he is devoted.

" Sir John Franklin and his party will
" have entered upon their third year before
" succour can penetrate amid the wastes of
" ice in which, in all probability, they are
" embedded, to guide them along the
" pampas of a frozen ocean, and restore
" them to earth. Sir John Richardson has
" proposed a plan which has been accepted
" by the Admiralty. We ask, is England
" to be content that our countrymen should
" only be sought by a heavy arctic caravan-
" sary under the conduct of an officer
" already in the wintry region of life?
" whose vigour of frame has departed,
" though not the vigour of that mind which
" won for him a justly high reputation?

" No! let her Majesty's ministers, with-
" out disturbing the expedition of which

" Sir John Richardson, strong in noble
" devotion, is to have the command, by the
" mere expenditure of some half-score
" hundreds of pounds, every month wasted
" on some fruitless experiment in our dock-
" yards, send forth an auxiliary party under
" charge of Dr. King, acting upon the plan
" he now proposes. Let them send forth
" this little band of venturous *voyageurs*,
" with Dr. King at their head, to shout
" the glad *halloo* of coming help along
" the desert plains, and amid the mountain
" bergs of the ice-bound world of waters.
" Thus let us prove that the lives of our
" enterprising countrymen are more dear
" to us than even clique and party-preju-
" dice and jobbing, dear as these are
" to the hearts of Englishmen,—a fact
" demonstrated in every act of public life,
" wherever we have influence, 'from pole
" 'to pole.'"

The *Medical Times*, 22nd December, '49.

" On the 10th of June, '47, a member of
" the medical profession, Dr. King, thus
" addresses Earl Grey:—'My Lord, one

" 'hundred and thirty-eight men are at
" 'this moment in imminent danger of
" 'perishing by famine.' Who is Dr.
" King? from whence proceeded the voice
" of warning which thus foreshadowed the
" two years and a half of most painful
" suspense which have passed?—Dr. King,
" in 1833, volunteered his services to ac-
" company Sir George Back, in a land
" journey, in search of the two Rosses—the
" uncle and nephew—who had made a
" voyage in search of the North-west
" Passage, and for the safety of whom ap-
" prehensions were entertained. Of the
" energy of character, boldness and pru-
" dence displayed by Dr. King, there never
" has been but one, and that a most fa-
" vourable opinion; further, there are many
" like ourselves who believe that quite as
" much of the guidance, safety, and general
" welfare of that expedition was due to the
" Physician as to the Commander. Dr.
" King is thus spoken of by Sir John
" Barrow, when alluding to the researches
" in natural history as some of the fruits of
" the expedition:—'It is impossible not to

" 'bestow the highest degree of praise on
" 'Dr. King, who with great exertion and
" 'diligence in collecting, and careful at-
" 'tention in preserving them, must have
" 'undergone much labour and constant
" 'anxiety.' Sir John Richardson passes
" the following encomium:—'These speci-
" 'mens were all prepared by Dr. King,
" 'who deserves the thanks of zoologists
" 'for devoting so much time and labour
" 'to the promotion of science.' Sir John
" Ross thus honourably alludes to Dr. King:
" —'I must do justice to the humane and
" 'praiseworthy intentions of Dr. King,
" 'and in the grateful remembrance of his
" 'noble conduct in volunteering to effect
" 'my rescue, the proposition which he
" 'has now made to Earl Grey is only what
" 'I might have expected. There is cer-
" 'tainly no person in every respect so
" 'eminently qualified to conduct that ser-
" 'vice as this enterprising individual.' A
" contemporary (The *Athenæum*) thus
" writes:—'It is incumbent on us to direct
" 'attention to the confirmation which
" 'Dr. King's views have already received,
" 'and the right which that circumstance

" 'unquestionably gives him to a hearing,
" 'wherever the measures best adapted for
" 'the recovery of Sir John Franklin and
" 'his band of adventurers have to be dis-
" 'cussed.'

" Two years and a half have now passed
" since Dr. King's warning, and no one
" knows whether The Franklin Expedition
" has been starved, or wrecked, or what
" has become of them. To the truth of
" their danger, Dr. King was a witness, as
" he was to the fact of the geographical
" mistakes and useless purposes of pre-
" ceding Polar Sea Expeditions.

" It was stated" (*Athenæum*, 24th Nov. '49,) " that the Council of the Royal
" Society had memorialised the Admiralty
" as to the expediency of summoning all
" the Arctic officers to its Councils, with
" the view of learning from them the best
" course to be pursued in resuming the
" interrupted search for Sir John Franklin.
" May *we* urge not *now* the *justice*, but
" the *expediency* of its not having forgotten
" Dr. King amongst the number of those
" consulted."

I proposed to the Government in 1836 to descend the Great Fish River to complete the survey of the unexplored coast of North America, to do by a *land journey* that which Sir John Franklin was dispatched to do by a *sea expedition*, a plan subsequently carried out by a private expedition, in command of that distinguished traveller, Mr. Thomas Simpson. The following testimony is, therefore, *apropos* for the search for Sir John Franklin:—

Spectator, 19th November, '36.

"That Dr. King's plan is bold will be "readily admitted; but it does not follow "that it is rash. With care and prudence, "dangers from man are not to be ap-"prehended; numbers have no power over "the rigour of the climate; and if the "gross quantity of food and other neces-"saries that can be carried is less, so is "the number amongst which they are to "be divided. Hearne made *his* discoveries "by plunging unattended amongst the "Indians; Mackenzie placed himself and "his few followers in a canoe, such as "Dr. King proposes to use; and the early

" navigators, whose exploration later ex-
" peditions have sailed to confirm, or fall
" short of, were badly victualled, in com-
" parative cockle shells. For in these, as
" in other affairs, the material means and
" appliances are of trivial consequence
" compared with the qualifications of the
" men who are to apply them."

Examiner, 20th November, '36.

" Dr. King is likely to realise an in-
" tention he has formed of resuming the
" research along the Northern coast of
" North America. We think him more
" than justified in some of his most hopeful
" and sanguine expectations,—and we wish
" him every possible success."

Morning Post, 23rd December, '36.

" We sincerely hope that Dr. King may
" be enabled to prosecute his hyperborean
" researches after his own economical and
" adventurous fashion. There can be no
" doubt of the zeal and capability of
" Dr. King,—the past is a guarantee for
" the future."

Globe, 20th November, '36.

" We wish the author every success in

" effecting his object of extending the coast
" line of North America; for which it is
" evident he possesses the requisite spirit
" of enterprise and resource."

Atlas, 20th November, '36.

" Dr. King's plan presents evident ad-
" vantages over all those that have been
" previously attempted, not only in the
" small amount of expenditure it will
" entail, but in the superior practicability
" of its operations. We hope he will be
" able to carry out a plan which seems so
" likely to eventuate in success."

Naval and Military Gazette, 19th February, '36.

" We have minutely inspected Dr. King's
" proposal, and find that he accompanied
" Sir George Back down the Great Fish
" River, and, moreover, being of the medi-
" cal profession, and well acquainted with
" the manners of the Canadian Voyagers,
" and the means of propitiating the native
" Indians, he appears well qualified to
" make the attempt with every prospect of
" success. We have the more confidence
" that he will succeed from the knowledge
" that five of his companions in the last

" expedition have volunteered to accompany
" him."

Sun, 15th February, '36.

" We have very minutely examined and " cross-examined all the circumstances con- " nected with Dr. King, and we have " conscientiously come to the conclusion " that he has established the very best " claims to success, so far as success is " attainable by manly daring, determined " enterprise, and absolute disregard of per- " sonal consequences. Dr. King is a gen- " tleman who unites in his own person " some of the best essentials for an under- " taking of this adventurous nature; he " possesses youth, health, medical and " scientific knowledge, experience of the " country and its inhabitants, a conciliatory " disposition, and, above all, a burning zeal " to have his name enrolled among those " who have already signalised themselves in " exploring the stormy regions of the North."

After all, the *best testimony* that can be adduced is that which comes from my companions in adventure down the Great Fish River in search of Sir J. Ross. It is true that Roderick McLeod, Charles Ross, and Peter Taylor are now numbered with the dead, but one of the most talented and public spirited proprietors and editors of the Press can vouch for the testimony; and I have that gentleman's permission to publish it.

York Factory, November 7th, 1836.

My dear King,—Here I am once again in the solitudes of the "Far West," cheerfully taking up the pen to write to you according to promise. London life is over! Where now are the snug parties—the theatres—your reflection—and the rest? All gone—sunk into endless night. Such are the strange vicissitudes of this fitful world.

When I parted with you at London Bridge I little anticipated the heavy forfeit I was about to pay for a winter in London. The place of my destination is Cumberland House, an appointment with which I have every reason to be pleased. My family have already preceded me hither, and to join them I'll have to travel the whole distance on snow shoes, which I may add to the other evils resulting from my journey to London.

Great changes have happened here since

you left. That incomprehensible disease[15], of which you heard so much while here, bids fair to make the place untenable. It returned last spring with redoubled violence. All your friends in the interior are just as you left them.

Now, my dear King, I long to learn how "affairs in general" have prospered with you—whether you still fondly cherish your Arctic journey—whether subscriptions[16] are fast filling up—and whether everything is cut and dry for a start. There are many here who would rejoice to see you among them again and again. There is a report that the Hudson Bay Company intend to prosecute it next year[17]. Peter Taylor is at Lac la Pluie, and fully expects you. Both he. as well as your other companions in adventure, are high in your praise, while Sir George Back is the theme of their aversion and contempt.

As no ships return from the country this season, this letter will reach you *viâ* New

[15] Influenza.

[16] I was endeavouring to raise, by public subscription, £.1000.——R. K.

[17] Mr. T. Simpson's Journey to the Polar Sea.

York, and, I fear, will cost a heavy postage, without affording any adequate return. But I have fulfilled your wish. Have you heard anything of Heron, or Stuart[18], and what is doing in the political world? Write me all this, and in return you shall have from me all you want, from a scull down to a periwinkle! I have hardly room to say that I always am, my dear King, yours most truly,

CHAS. ROSS.

To Dr. King, M.D.

Great Slave Lake, July 2, 1836.

My dear King,—Both your letters of last September came duly to hand, and I was extremely happy to learn of your welfare. May you long enjoy that blessing is my sincere wish.

Your determination to accomplish the discovery of the North-West Passage inspires me with the hope of seeing you the current season, and if your plans admit of your coming this length to pass the ensuing winter, it will be to me most agreeable. Even if the upper establishment[19] should be

[18] The discoverer of Fraser's River.

[19] Athabasca Lake.

your residence, some very calamitous event must intervene to prevent me from going to see you.

It may, perhaps, be in favour of your enterprise, the late intimacy that has taken place between the Chipewyan and Esquimaux tribes, in the course of the last summer, on the Thlew-ee[20]. Amongst the latter there were many inhabitants of the Thlew-ee-cho[21]; but the majority were those that frequent Churchill annually, to prove which they produced the articles they obtained from the Hudson Bay Company in the way of trade, and readily exchanged the same with their guests, by way of cementing their friendship. There can be no doubt of a successful issue to your undertaking, of which I feel so confident that I hail with pleasure the moment that will bring you once more among us, as I am equally certain that every attention will be directed to promote your views, and be assured none shall more willingly contribute thereto than your humble servant.

I have not succeeded in obtaining the skeleton of a moose-deer, but I have bright

[20] Fish River. [21] Great Fish River.

hopes of getting it, as well as a skeleton of a musk ox, by the next spring; and if you do not make your appearance, I shall endeavour to forward them to England to your address.

I am much obliged to you for your kind wishes to myself and family; they are, thank God, in the enjoyment of health, and unite their wishes to mine for your welfare and prosperity.

Believe me, my dear KING,

Your sincere friend,

ALEX. R. M'LEOD.

To Dr. KING, M.D.

Norway House, 12th August, 1836.

DEAR SIR,—I was very happy to receive your letter last spring, when I arrived at Norway House, always expecting to see you here again. I was here for about a month and a half, looking earnestly for your arrival. I was at last obliged to join with the expedition again[22], and I am now going to Red River, where I shall remain until the first ice, and then travel to Athabasca to join with the rest. M'Kay and Sinclair have joined it. Of the birds

[22] Mr. T. Simpson's "Journey to the Polar Sea."

and insects you requested me to preserve for you, I have got as many as I could.

Dear Sir, I should have been very happy to have seen you here, and joined with you with all my heart, but since it cannot be, I therefore must leave you, with my best wishes for your temporal and eternal welfare.

I remain,

Your sincere friend and humble Servant,

PETER TAYLOR.

To Dr. King, M.D.

Athabusca Fort, 28th May, 1837.

Dear Sir,—I was very sorry to hear that you could not get into the country last spring, for I was at Norway House waiting till you should be there; and when I saw you were not coming, I was obliged to enter into the service of the expedition. But I was most sorry when I received your last letter[28] that you sent by the last ship—though I hope I shall have the pleasure of seeing you in the North if you do come.

Your ever true friend,

PETER TAYLOR.

To Dr. King, M.D.

[28] Informing him of Sir George Back's ill-starred voyage in the "Terror," in lieu of my Polar Land journey.

THE FRANKLIN EXPEDITION.

12th Dec. '44, the Board of Admiralty, resolved upon another expedition by sea in search of the North-West Passage, and appointed to the command Sir John Franklin, then fifty-eight years of age.

The Erebus and Terror, ships of 378 and 326 tons, were selected by the Admiralty for this service, having earned a reputation in the Antarctic as well as Arctic Regions by no means creditable to them, in command of Sir James Ross and Sir George Back.

The instructions to Sir John Franklin, signed on behalf of the Admiralty, Haddington; G. Cockburn; W. H. Gage; 5th May, '45, comprise 316 lines divided into 23 paragraphs; but all we have to deal with runs thus:—

" Lancaster Sound and its continuation

" through Barrow Strait, having been " four times navigated by Sir Edward " Parry, and since by whaling ships, will " probably be found without any obstacles " from ice or islands, and Sir Edward Parry " having also proceeded from the latter in " a straight course to Melville Island, it " is hoped that the remaining portion of " the passage, about 900 miles, to Behring " Strait, may also be found equally free " from obstruction; and in proceeding to " the Westward, therefore, you will not " stop to examine any openings either to " the Northward or Southward in that " Strait, but continue to push to the West- " ward without loss of time in the latitude " of about 74¼°, till you have reached the " longitude of that portion of land on " which Cape Walker is situated. From " that point we desire that every effort " be used to endeavour to penetrate to the " Southward and Westward in a course " as direct towards Behring Strait, as the " position and extent of the ice, or the " existence of land, may admit. But " should your progress be arrested by ice

" of a permanent appearance, and that
" when passing the mouth of the Strait,
" between Devon and Cornwallis Islands,
" you had observed that it was open and
" clear of ice, we desire that you will duly
" consider whether that channel might not
" offer a more practicable outlet from the
" Archipelago and a more ready access to
" the open sea."

Fully satisfied that Sir John Franklin was destined to lead a "forlorn hope," I addressed Lord Stanley, now Lord Derby, then Secretary of State for the Colonies, in these terms:—

" 17, *Savile Row*, 20*th February*, 1845.

" My Lord,—As it is determined to
" prosecute the discovery of the North-west
" Passage by sea from East to West, I can
" fairly approach your Lordship to propose
" for adoption the following plan for a land
" journey:—

" I propose that a party of two officers,
" one of the medical profession, a boat
" carpenter, and thirteen men fully equip-
" ped for the service, should leave Montreal

" in Canada, sufficiently early to reach the " Athabasca Lake in July. Here half the " baggage should be left, and the boat " carpenter and two men should remain, in " order to build a boat 28 feet long—an " occupation of three weeks. The ex- " plorers should then proceed to the head " waters of the Fish River to fix upon an " eligible position to winter. The route to " the Fish River from the Athabasca Lake " is well known to the Indians and fur " traders, and is minutely described in " 'King's Journey to the Arctic Ocean " 'by the Great Fish River.' The " winter establishment fixed, one officer " and five men, with an Indian guide, " should return to the Athabasca Lake; " and having despatched the boat carpenter " with the Indian guide and the two men " to the Fish River party, there to build a " second boat, proceed in the newly-built " boat *viâ* the Slave and Mackenzie Rivers " to the Great Bear Lake, the wintering " post of two of the overland journeys. " The parties—which, for convenience, it " will be as well to call the eastern and

" western party—having securely housed
" themselves, should at once adapt their
" means to their ends in getting through
" the winter and providing for the future.
" To collect and hoard provisions, and to
" pave the way to the Polar Sea, so as to
" be on its shores as early as the navigation
" will permit, and to observe all and every-
" thing in the vast field before them, are
" the main features of an Arctic winter
" with a land party. The western party
" will be further occupied in transporting
" —as the traveller Simpson—their boat
" to the Coppermine River, and the eastern
" party their boat to the Great Fish River.
" As soon as these rivers are open the
" Expedition must be in progress; the one
" detachment for Cape Britannia or Ripon
" Island, as it was once called, and the
" other for Victoria Land,—the one to
" ascertain the connection of the mainland
" with that of North Somerset or of
" Melville Peninsula, and if the former,
" the character of its western land; and
" the other to trace Victoria Land westerly,
" with the view of testing its value re-

" latively to the North-west Passage. To " enter further into detail is unnecessary " until the service is determined upon; but " in order that my ability to supply the " minutest detail may not be questioned, I " take leave to state that I led the mission " in search of Sir John Ross not only into " but out of the Polar Regions.

" It cannot be questioned that the " knowledge of such a journey as I propose " being in progress from East to West, " under a determined leader, would mainly " assist in raising that moral courage " which is requisite in pushing an adven- " turous way through an unknown sea. In " two instances, journeys by land have been " set in motion to aid expeditions by sea. " As it now stands, Sir John Franklin " will have to 'take the ice'—as the push- " ing through an ice-blocked sea is termed " in utter ignorance of the extent of his " labours; and, in case of difficulty, with " certainly no better prospect before him " than that which befel Sir John Ross, " whose escape from a perilous position of " four years' standing is admitted by all to

" have been almost miraculous. I have " contended against the present attempt by " sea from an honest conviction of its " impracticability in the present state of " our knowledge of Arctic lands; and, " except the journey which I propose is " undertaken, it is no difficult matter to " foresee that the grand problem will " actually be in abeyance. My position " now is very different to that of 1836. " I was then unknown; and from the sim- " plicity and economy of my views con- " sidered a visionary. Nine years have " altered the state of things. The views " put forward by me in 1836 in favour of a " land journey have been verified; the " Sea Expedition in the Terror has failed; " and the little band of adventurers, " led by the most successful of the Polar " travellers, the intrepid Simpson,—after " my own economical fashion,—have aston- " ished the most sanguine geographers of " the day. Well pleased should I have " been if that intelligent traveller had " lived to complete his task, so ably " begun; and then he who is now ad-

" dressing your Lordship would not have " intruded himself upon your notice. It " cannot be denied that I was mainly " instrumental in directing the spirit of " enterprise again to the North, at a " period when Sir John Ross and Sir " George Back were fresh before the " Government—and in face of their " testimony 'that there were fewer temp- " 'tations than ever for making any fresh " 'attempts at solving the great geo- " 'graphical problem of three centuries:' " and my restless activity on this subject " continued until the 'ill-starred voyage in " 'the Terror,' in command of Sir George " Back, and the successful land journey " in command of Mr. Simpson, were deter- " mined upon. My last effort in regard to " the Expedition in the Terror closed with " the words:—'That those who were " 'sanguine as to the success of that enter- " 'prise would be grievously mistaken; " 'and should that insane portion of the " 'instructions, the crossing the isthmus " 'dividing the waters of Wager Bay from " 'Regent Inlet, be attempted, the most

" 'disastrous results might be expected.' " How far I was correct the Government " has sad proof. Although I do not cherish " the most distant idea of again having an " opportunity of pleading in favour of a " Land Journey, under my own charge,— " seeing that I have pleaded nine years in " vain,—I am as alive as ever to the pro- " gress of arctic discovery; and I do hope " that your Lordship will entertain the " plan here submitted. Your Lordship " will have no difficulty in finding volunteers " for such a service; but in order to meet " any difficulty of this nature, I am ready " to volunteer the whole command, or part " of the command with any officer your " Lordship may appoint, provided that he " is of my own age and in possession of the " same amount of physical capability. I " have the honour to be, &c.

" RICHARD KING.

" *To* The Right Honourable Lord Stanley."

Sir John Franklin was last heard of on the 26th of July of the year of his departure in latitude 74° and longitude 66° of Baffin Bay. On the 10th June, '47, therefore, I thus addressed Earl Grey, who filled the post of Secretary of State for the Colonies in the place of Lord Stanley:—

17, *Savile Row*, 10*th June*, 1847.

My Lord,—One hundred and thirty-eight men are at this moment in imminent danger of perishing from famine. Sir John Franklin's Expedition to the North Pole in 1845, as far as we know, has never been heard of from the moment it sailed. An attempt to save our countrymen, if not by the all-powerful efforts of Government, by the ever-watchful British public will be made. The exploring party were well aware of this when they started; for they knew that Sir John Ross was not allowed to die the death of famine, nor Colonel Conolly and Captain Stoddart that of the sword, without an effort being made for their relief. I trust, my Lord, the British Government are now fully aware of the wishes of the public in regard to the lives of their men of travel and of war. If the course adopted since Queen

Elizabeth's time, in regard to Polar Discovery Expeditions, has hitherto been one of profound secrecy scarcely worthy the honourable service in which they have been engaged—and no one knows whither the one hundred and thirty-eight lost men were intended to wander, for all is at this moment conjecture beyond the walls of the Admiralty,—in future let the service be one of public competition; and let the attempt that is to be made to save Sir John Franklin from his hard fate, in Christian charity, be made fully public, that the proposed plans, —for there will doubtless be several,—may be discussed, and therein be raised a praiseworthy competition, which will, at all events, have the semblance of an endeavour to follow the right course. It is greatly to be regretted that Lord Stanley did not entertain the plan which I proposed for acting by land in concert with Sir John Franklin's expedition by sea. It is scarcely possible that the two services could have missed each other; therefore there would not have been that anxiety for the fate of Sir John Franklin which now exists, nor the necessity which is now paramount for the most active and energetic exertions for his rescue.

I take leave to address your Lordship under three heads. The probable position of the Polar Expedition; the condition of the Polar lands about it; and the best means of saving it.

In the outset I have a difficulty, owing to the route of Sir John Franklin not having been officially announced. Sir John Barrow, in his private capacity, has, however, stated in his History of Arctic Voyages, "that it "is by Barrow Strait and the Sea washing "North Somerset on the one side, and Banks "and Wollaston Land on the other;"—which may be presumed to be correct, as he was the official who drew up the orders given to Sir John Franklin on his departure.

The position, then, that I should assign to the lost Expedition is the Western land of North Somerset—the midway between the settlements of the Hudson's Bay Company on the Mackenzie and the fishing grounds of the whalers in Barrow Strait. If Sir John Franklin has attempted to make a short cut westward, instead of sailing southward along the western land of North Somerset, and wrecked himself on Banks and Wollaston Land,—he has run headlong into that danger of which I expressly warned him in the following words:—" If we direct " our attention to the movements of the " various Polar Sea Expeditions, which " have been set afloat since 1818, we find " that in every instance the difficulties " arose from the same cause,—the clinging " to lands having an eastern aspect. Sir " Edward Parry, in his Second Expedition, " made attempts for two successive summers " to penetrate the eastern entrance of the " Fury and Hecla Strait,—and failed; and " in his Third Expedition, he lost the Fury " while pushing his way along the eastern " land of North Somerset. Sir John Ross, " in his Second Expedition, was four years " advancing four miles along the same " eastern land; and was at last obliged to " abandon his vessel. Captain Lyon and " Sir G. Back made, separately, unsuccessful " attempts to reach Repulse Bay,—which " has an eastern aspect. How, it may be "inquired, is this general difficulty to be "avoided? By taking the road which is "fairly open to us,—the lands that have a "western aspect."

If, however, Banks and Wollaston Land should form the resting-place of the Erebus and Terror, it will not be that of the Expedition. If the party have kept together (and woe be to them if they have not!) they will take to their boats and make for the western land of North Somerset, for the double purpose of reaching Barrow Strait in search of the northern whalers, as Sir John Ross did successfully, and the Great Fish River in search of Esquimaux for provision,—or for letter conveyance to the Copper Indians, with whom the Esquimaux are now in friendly relation. It is to the western land of North Somerset that we must direct our attention—to that spot we must bend our course.

North Somerset is a peninsula, forming the north-eastern corner of North America, the western shore of Regent Inlet, and the eastern shore of the Great Fish River estuary. At least, such it is represented to us by Sir

John Ross,—and such I believe it to be; for the evidence in favour of it is very convincing, while that which has been adduced against it is mere conjecture. In a practical point of view, however, it is of very little moment whether the character of North Somerset is insular or peninsular; and I can therefore spare your Lordship's time by avoiding to give you proof of this,—which would fill a volume, in consequence of the importance that has been put upon it, in support of the theory of a North-West Passage at the bottom of Regent Inlet.

The western land of North Somerset can easily be reached by a party travelling overland from Canada; and it cannot be denied that a land journey affords the only sure mode of *extending* our geographical knowledge, and therefore the only sure *ladder* by which to reach Sir John Franklin. In practice, however, it is necessary to know whether the question mooted has science or humanity in view; for, in the former case, it is argued that expeditions by sea are the best, and in the latter journeys by land; although there is always tacked on to these even larger promises of advancement to geographical science than is made in the other. I confess I could never understand the logic of the argument; but it is not less a matter of truth—for the scientific expedition which Sir John Franklin now commands was set afloat in the face of the following facts; that seven of the ten Polar Sea expeditions could be thus briefly described. Capt. Lyon's expedition was modestly called by him "An unsuccessful attempt to reach Repulse Bay;" in the body of the narrative of Sir G. Back's expedition will be found the same tale which Capt. Lyon gave on his title-page; Capt. Ross returned after four years wintering, without advancing a step towards the object in view; Capt. Parry failed in his attempt to reach the Polar Sea by Regent Inlet; Capt. Beechey saw the Polar Sea, and that is all; and Capt. Buchan was not so fortunate as Capt. Beechey;—while a short survey of the polar land journeys affords a standard of comparison and develops the true position. The journey of Hearne proved the existence of a Polar Sea, and demonstrated that it could be reached overland by way of Canada;

and the success which attended Sir John Franklin's first polar land journey proved that the opinion which had been formed was in every way correct. The distance between the Coppermine River and Point Turnagain was thus made known to us. A second polar land journey added to our knowledge of the coast line the distance between the Mackenzie and the Coppermine Rivers, and as far westward of the Mackenzie as Foggy Island; which far surpassed in extent the prosperous voyage of Sir Edward Parry in 1819 and 1820. A third polar land journey eclipsed all, and left to be surveyed but a small portion of the North American boundary of the Polar Sea. The fruits of the ten Polar Sea Expeditions will not balance with those of one of the Polar Land Journeys; and the harvest of the first and the least successful of these interesting missions is greater than that which remains to be gathered. Even the little that has been done by the Polar Sea Expeditions is of doubtful character.—Banks Land, the North Georgian Group of islands and the boundaries of Barrow Strait are still problems; in fact, so many lesser puzzles as additions to the great geographical puzzle of three centuries. It is not so with the labours of the commanders of the Polar Land Journeys. The footing which they made is permanent; while Croker Mountains have dissolved, and islands threaten to be continents, and continents islands—the natural consequence of discovery in ships.

It is altogether illogical to suppose that a party isolated from the known world, as Sir John Franklin is at this moment, can reach civilization with as great facility as a party from the known world can reach him. Sir John Franklin, if he can keep his party together, will rest where he is, and daily look for assistance from his home. This was a subject which the promoters of the Expedition in search of Sir John Ross had to prove in 1833; and nothing has since occurred to create a different opinion.

There are manifestly two modes of attempting to afford Sir John Franklin relief—to convey provision to him and convey him to the provision; but I shall have no difficulty in proving to your Lordship that there is but one mode practicable,—that of conveying him to the provision. The conveyance of provision to Sir John Ross was a failure—and in that case it was only contemplated to relieve a small party of twenty-three men—for this evident reason, that the country is too poor to support a large party—and a large party it is necessary to have, when every kind of provision has to be carried on men's backs over the innumerable obstructions which are to be met with in an overland journey.

The party in search of Sir John Ross saved themselves from starvation by consuming the food intended for that gallant officer long before they had reached the half-way house to him. These are not mere assertions to suit the moment; for the facts which support these opinions were recorded in 1836, in "King's Journey to the Arctic "Ocean by the Great Fish River," in these words;—"Although overland expeditions "towards the northern coast of North "America may be regarded as less expen-"sive and less dangerous than an arctic "voyage, and more likely to obtain acces-"sions to science and commerce, they may

" greatly vary amongst themselves in all " these respects, according to the mode in " which they may be undertaken. They " may, however, be all comprised in two " classes. To the first class belong small " companies, travelling with the least pos- " sible incumbrance, and strictly adopting " the mode of proceeding and the means of " subsistence in use amongst the natives of " the country and the traders who visit " them. Individuals uniting physical " ability, both for doing and suffering, " necessary to meet the dangers and " fatigues of this mode of travelling, with " talents and acquirements necessary to " render their journey availing for the " purposes of science, have already effected " much at a very trifling outlay. Hearne " and Mackenzie prove the truth of this " assertion. The second class consists of " those expeditions which possess a more " organised and systematic form; being " composed of a company of men and " officers accustomed to military or naval " service,—seldom or never amounting to a " smaller number than three officers and

" twenty men; and consequently requiring
" a considerable amount of baggage. For
" the conveyance of these men and their
" stores the small canoes of the country,
" which are readily made, repaired, and
" transported, are quite inadequate. Boats
" of larger dimensions are therefore had
" recourse to; which are easily damaged,
" are with difficulty repaired, and are too
" cumbrous to be conveyed across the
" portages when the distance is great or
" the ground uneven. These evils are not
" theoretical; they have been proved by
" fearful experience, and have been the
" cause of immense difficulty or failure:—
" for though they form but a small military
" troop, they are too large to travel with
" advantage through a country in which
" the means of subsistence are very scanty
" and still more precarious. The diffi-
" culties which they have to encounter
" are infinitely increased when the indivi-
" duals comprising the company are not
" practically acquainted with the mode of
" travelling through the district to be
" crossed, and consequently cannot be

"separated from each other without the "greatest danger of fatally losing their "way; on which account they cannot seek "game and other sources of subsistence. "From want of experience they are unable "either to bear the burdens or travel the "distance which a Canadian or an Indian "would disregard. Time, the most important element in northern expeditions, is "inevitably lost, and neither the energy "nor the genius of the commanding officer "can retrieve the error when the season is "advanced upon them[1]."

The evidence which I have brought forward I most conscientiously believe to be conclusive, that the means to be adopted for relieving Sir John Franklin will be for the Government to despatch one or more vessels with provision to the western land of North Somerset by Barrow Strait in the summer of 1848, and to call upon the Hudson Bay Company to use their best exertions to fill their northern depôts with pemican, dried meat and fish by the same date. Informa-

[1] "Journey to the Arctic Ocean by the Great Fish "River, by Dr. King, M.D.," pp. 293-298.

tion of such provision having been made should be conveyed, in the course of the summer of 1848, by a small party provided with Indian guides—in case it should be desirable to convey the lost party to the Hudson Bay depôts on the Mackenzie or the Great Slave Lake, instead of to the southern boundary of Barrow Strait in search of the provision vessels. Such a party, my Lord, I will undertake to lead, in company with any officer the Government may appoint, provided he be of my own age and in possession of the same amount of physical capability. I am induced to volunteer my services because I believe that I am the only person in whom the requisites for such a journey are to be found. Sir John Richardson counts twice the number of years that I do, and he is not acquainted with either the country or the American Indians to the extent that I am;—and I should disgrace myself as an Englishman if I did not step forward to save a veteran in the service like him from the necessity of fulfilling his promise to the Admiralty of going in search of Sir John

Franklin in March next in case of our receiving no tidings of him in the autumn of this year. The Government surely cannot consent that Sir John Richardson, arrived at an age much better suited to receive honour than to endure hardship, should expose himself to fresh dangers and privations, when there are the young and the competent anxious to take their turn.

If Sir John Franklin is to be relieved, it must be in the summer of 1848. He must be spared the winter of that year;—and the Government will incur a heavy responsibility if every effort that experience can suggest is not made to save him from such an ordeal—which can scarcely be contemplated without the most painful feelings. Sir John Franklin's expedition should not have set sail, in face of the facts I laid before the late Government; and the least that the present Government can do is to lessen the evils that their predecessors have allowed the veteran to heap upon himself. And it will certainly not be taking the best means to send one veteran in search of another.

In conclusion, my Lord, I would call your attention to the opinions of the medical officers of the second expedition of Sir Edward Parry in answer to the query of that gallant commander—" As to the probable effect " that a third winter passed in the Arctic " regions would produce on the health of " the officers, seamen, and marines under his " charge." Mr. Edwards and Mr. Skeoch report, " that during the last winter and " subsequently, the aspect of the crew of the " Fury in general, together with the increased " number and character of the complaints, " strongly indicated that the peculiarity of " the climate and service was slowly effect- " ing a serious decay of their constitutional " powers[2];" and Captain Lyon remarks, that " He has for some time been of opinion " that the Fury's passing a third winter in " the country would be extremely hazardous. " He is induced thus to express himself " from the great change he has observed in " the constitution of the officers and men " of the Hecla, and by the appearance of " some very severe cases of scurvy since the " summer has commenced. Long continu-

[2] Parry's Second Voyage, p. 471.

" ance on one particular diet, almost total " deprivation of fresh animal and vegetable " food for above two years, and the neces- " sary and close confinement for several " months of each severe winter, are un- " doubtedly the causes of the general altera- " tion of constitution which has for some time " past been so evident. He therefore conceives " that a continued exposure to the same " deprivations and confinement, and the " painful monotony of a third winter to " men whose health is precarious, would " in all probability be attended with very " serious consequences[3]." Notwithstanding these opinions so strongly expressed, Sir John Franklin must pass a third winter in the polar regions if there are no tidings of him in the autumn; but I trust, my Lord, that you will not allow him to contend with a fourth, without giving me an opportunity of rendering him the only succour which has the probability of success,—that of being the messenger of the information where provisions are stored for him.

I have the honour to be, my Lord, &c.

RICHARD KING.

[3] Parry's Second Voyage, p. 473.

Again.

To the Right Hon. Earl Grey.

17, *Savile Row*, 25*th November*, 1847.

The last ray of hope has passed when Sir John Franklin by his own exertions can save himself and his one hundred and thirty-seven followers from the death of starvation. I trust, therefore, your Lordship will excuse my calling your attention to my letter of the 10th of June last, which is acknowledged, but remains unanswered. I should not have intruded myself again on your Lordship's notice were I able to believe that your Lordship is fully sensible of the heavy responsibility which the calamity has placed upon you. The Admiralty Board may send assistance by the Atlantic and Pacific Oceans—they may set in motion every mariner who has assisted in ploughing the northern seas,—yet it will not relieve you from responsibility as the principal Secretary of State for the Colonies. The service which I have proposed, as a matter of precedent, should emanate from the Colonial Board. It was from that

Board that assistance was despatched in search of Sir John Ross; and from that Board the Polar Land Journeys, so fruitful in result, were one and all set on foot.

I have already called your Lordship's attention to the evidence which Sir Edward Parry, on his retirement from active service, has laid before the Admiralty, in confirmation of his opinion that the most serious consequences to his crew would be the result of passing a third winter in the Polar regions,—and a third winter, it is now too evident, the lost expedition must pass in the inclement North. In order, however, to save our fellow creatures from all the horrors of starvation and its awful consequences, I have offered to your Lordship to undertake the boldest journey which has ever been proposed,—and one which is justifiable only from the circumstances. I have offered to attempt to reach the western land of North Somerset before the close of the summer of 1848,—to accomplish, in fact, in one summer that which has never been accomplished under two summers;—by which means I incur the risk of having to winter with the Esquimaux,—or of having to make the journey along the barren ground to winter quarters on snow shoes. How, your Lordship may inquire, is this Herculean task to be performed? Upon what grounds do I rest my hope of success? I would state, in answer, that it is necessary the leader of such a journey should have an intimate knowledge of the country and the people through which he has to pass,—the health to stand the rigour of the climate, and the strength to undergo the fatigue of mind and body to which he will be subjected. It is because I have these requisites, which I conscientiously believe are not to be found in another, that I hope to effect my purpose. The uncivilised man,—and upon the service under consideration we must have large dealings with him,—in choosing his subject looks for physical, not mental, qualifications; and if these are not apparent, he is cautious and undecided,—and the more you hurry him the less certain you are of making him answer your purpose. Time, the most important element in Polar travelling, will in this way be lost to the stranger in the land, and the journey rendered unavailing; while my great activity, power of endurance, and success as a physician, during my journey in search of Sir John Ross, must be fresh in the recollection of nine-tenths of the Indian population through which such a mission as I have proposed will have to pass,—and cannot fail to secure to me every co-operation. It is a well ascertained fact that the medical traveller succeeds where all others fail.

If your Lordship will take a glance at the map of North America, and direct your attention to but three places; Behring Strait on the Pacific, Barrow Strait on the Atlantic, and the land of North Somerset between them, you will perceive that to render assistance to a party situated on that land there are two ways by sea and one by land. Of the two sea ways, the route by the Pacific is altogether out of the question. It is an idea of by-gone days; while that by the Atlantic is so doubtful of success that it is merely necessary, in order to put this assistance aside as far from certain, to mention that Sir John Ross found Barrow Strait closed in the summer of 1832; and, as the Strait has been visited only six times, it may be far from an unusual circumstance. To a land journey, then, alone we can look for success;—for the failure of a land journey would be the exception to the rule, while the failure of a sea expedition would be the rule itself. To the western land of North Somerset, where, I maintain, Sir John Franklin will be found, the Great Fish River is the direct and only route; and although the approach to it is through a country too poor and too difficult of access to admit of the transport of provision, it may be made the medium of communication between the lost expedition and the civilised world; and Indian guides be thus placed at their disposal to convey them to the hunting grounds of the Red Men. Without such guides it is impossible that they can reach these hunting grounds. It was by that intricate and dangerous river that I reached the Polar Sea while acting as second officer in search of Sir John Ross; and as there were but two officers on that honourable service, your Lordship can but look to those officers for the elements of success, if a mission by that river is resolved upon. All that I can do, as one of those officers so peculiarly circumstanced, is to place my views on record as an earnest of my sincerity. Even if the Admiralty should determine to try to force provision-vessels through Behring and Barrow Straits, and scour the vicinity in boats for the lost expedition,—and try they must,—and succeed, it will be satisfactory to know that such a mission as I have proposed was adopted; while if they should fail in their attempts—and I am sorry to say that I fully believe they will fail—and the service under consideration is put aside, it will be a source of regret that not only the nation at large will feel, but the whole civilised world. When this regret is felt, and every soul has perished, such a mission as I have proposed will be urged again and again for adoption; for it is impossible that the country will rest satisfied until a search be made for the remains of the lost expedition by a person in whom the country has confidence. No inexperienced person can go upon such an errand. The efforts of the Danish Government for the lost colonies of Greenland, the efforts of the Portuguese Government for the brothers Cotereal, and the efforts of the French Government for the unfortunate La Perouse, cannot fail to raise our national pride when placed in similar circumstances.

It has been stated in the periodical literature of the day that a party of sappers and miners sailed last June in charge of provisions destined for the Mackenzie River, as supplies for the lost expedition; and that Sir John Richardson is to leave England in February next to head this party. I hope this may be mere report. Such an expedition would be one of relief from a difficulty which, to be successful, anticipates the difficulty to be overcome; for if the lost expedition can reach the Mackenzie River, or even the Great Bear Lake by the Coppermine River, to benefit by these supplies, they have solved the problem of more than three centuries,—they have discovered the North-west Passage, a dream we can scarcely expect to be realised.

The recent survey of Dr. Rae is satisfactory only so far as it confirms the Esquimaux chart furnished to Sir John Ross; and as it supports my views, that the western shore of the Great Fish River estuary is continuous with the western land of North Somerset,—or, to use my own words of 1836, " that from Cape Hay the land trends " N.N.E., when it dips the horizon, where " a small space intervenes—in all probability a deep bay—to a land gradually " rising into boldness, following a north-" westerly course, the extremes of which " are named Points Ross and Booth[4]." If the survey of Dr. Rae could be depended upon, the view I have taken is the correct one, but at present it is valueless in a geographical point of view. The peninsularity of North Somerset is still a problem; for it is far from evident that Dr. Rae reached Lord Mayor Bay of Sir John Ross. He not only neglected to search for the wreck of the Victory steam-ship or some token of Sir John Ross's footing, but he commenced his journey without providing him-

[4] "Journey to the Arctic Ocean, by the Great Fish River, by Dr. King, M.D.," vol. ii. p. 26.

self with the means to correct his longitude, —which he calculated entirely by dead reckoning. Further, he not only made his survey when all nature was clothed in ice and snow—which placed it out of his power at all times to recognise land from water, much more to distinguish that water which was salt from that which was fresh—but he made short cuts to save a journey round capes and bays, and thus lost sight of the continuity of land, which an experienced traveller would not have done.

Even under the most favourable circumstances, it is impossible to put any other than a low value upon a winter survey in the Polar regions. This is exemplified in the journey which Sir James Ross made across the isthmus of Boothia, when he not only traced a large portion of land under an impression that he was travelling along the continent of America, which, after several years was found by a summer survey to have been an island, but he actually passed by the estuary of the Great Fish River, altogether unaware of the existence of that magnificent stream. Poctes' Bay was the name given by Sir James Ross to the estuary into which the Great Fish River has since been found to empty itself.

Dr. Rae has, however, furnished us with some interesting matter for discussion. For instance, there is the evidence of the outlet of the Fish River into Regent Inlet—for which I have so long contended; and the fact that the failure of his enterprise is wholly attributable to an accumulation of ice upon an eastern land gives additional weight to the law which I have established, that all arctic lands that have an eastern aspect are ice-clogged. The journey which I proposed to Lord Glenelg in 1835, afterwards to Lord Stanley, and which I now, at the expiration of twelve years, propose to your Lordship—is along a land which has a western aspect, and which I have shewn is almost invariably ice-free. My progress, therefore, to the spot where I suppose the lost expedition will be found will be unimpeded; and not only will the question as to the peninsularity of North Somerset be set at rest, but that which remains undone of the northern configuration of America will be completed,—for it is by hugging the western land of North Somerset only that we can expect to fall upon the traces of the lost expedition, if we are to look for it in that direction.

I would state, in conclusion, that the various surveys which have been set afloat since I came forward in 1836 as a volunteer have but cleared the way to render the soundness of my views the more apparent. The several expeditions which have since been undertaken, whether they have resulted in success or failure, have afforded so many successive links in the chain of evidence which demonstrates the scientific character of the views advanced by me in 1836,—and for adherence to which I have been refused all character as a scientific traveller and all honorary acknowledgment of faithful service to my country. I am not, however, asking your Lordship to recommend to Her Majesty the bestowing upon me a mark of approbation, as a reward for the soundness of these views, which has been bestowed upon those who contradicted them. I am asking your Lordship to appoint me to a service for which I am peculiarly qualified,—a service of extreme hazard and labour, but which, to be successful, must be undertaken by some one of great experience. I am willing to labour still for that recognition which will give me equality with those who are now my superiors;—and when I state to your Lordship that I stand alone as a single individual, isolated from the heroes of the Pole in regard to reward for services, I trust your Lordship will consider that I have strong claims for such a service. The time has arrived, I say, when I am able to refer your Lordship to my past services and my present character as a guarantee that I am sincere in my offer, and as an earnest that I will faithfully discharge the duties which will devolve upon me if I should be honoured with the service I am seeking at your Lordship's hands. Surely, my Lord, I should now have a peace offering. A considerable portion of the main continent of North America bears the outline which I gave to it,—in which I differed with Sir George Back. The Great Bay of Simpson and the trending of the land north-east of

Cape Hay are so many truths, and although the trending of the land named Points Ross and Booth—which I maintain runs N.W. and S.E., and not East and West as Sir George Back has mapped it—and the peninsularity of North Somerset, for which I have for twelve years contended, have to be proved, they are rendered highly probable by the journey of Dr. Rae.

That I have laboured through this difficult subject for so many years, and at last successfully—that I have been the first to shew how the great puzzle of three centuries could be unravelled—and that I have constantly offered for a period of twelve of those years, whenever an opportunity occurred, to be the means of unravelling it—inspire me with the hope that I shall at last find justice at the hands of your Lordship, and that I may be allowed to have my place in the great effort which must be made for the rescue of the one hundred and thirty-eight men who compose the lost Expedition.—I have the honour, &c.

RICHARD KING.

Again.

To the Right Hon. Earl Grey.

17, *Savile Row, Dec.* 8, 1847.

MY LORD,—Since my letter to your Lordship of the 25th of November, the *Athenæum* has published, on high authority, the effort which the Board of Admiralty has resolved to make in search of the Polar Sea Expedition under the command of Sir John Franklin. By that effort the field which I have proposed to your Lordship is by no means rendered unnecessary; while it is shewn to be important from the fact, that if Sir John Richardson fails in finding the lost Expedition along the coast of North America comprised between the Mackenzie and the Coppermine Rivers, or Wollaston Land, which is opposite to that coast, he is to search Victoria Land in the summer of 1849.

Victoria Land can as easily be reached from the Great Fish River as the western land of North Somerset. I can search, therefore, that locality in the first instance, if it be considered necessary;—especially as it is known that our lost countrymen will have ceased to exist before Sir John Richardson can make the proposed search. I see no reason, however, to alter my opinion, expressed to your Lordship in my letter of the 10th of June last, in these words:—" If " that land should prove the resting-place of " the Erebus and Terror, it will not be that " of the Expedition. If the party have kept " together, they will take to their boats " and make for the western land of North " Somerset,—for the double purpose of " reaching Barrow Strait in search of " whalers, as Sir John Ross did successfully, " and the Great Fish River Estuary for " provisions or letter conveyance to the " Copper Indians, with whom the Esquimaux " are now in friendly relation."

The fact, that all lands which have a western aspect are generally ice-free—which I dwelt largely upon when the Expedition sailed—must have had weight with Sir John Franklin; he will, therefore, on finding himself in a serious difficulty while pushing along the eastern side of Victoria Land, at once fall upon the western land of North Somerset as a refuge.

The "effort" by Behring Strait and Banks Land is praiseworthy in attempt, but "forlorn in hope,"—and may be dealt with briefly. In the former effort it is assumed that Sir John Franklin has made the "Passage," and that his "arrest is between "the Mackenzie River and Icy Cape;" in the latter, that Sir James Ross will reach Banks Land, and trace its continuity to Victoria or Wollaston Land—and thus make the "Passage."

In the first place, we have no reason to believe that Sir John Franklin and Sir James Ross will be more fortunate than their predecessors; and if we can indulge such fond hopes, we cannot trust to them. In the second place, we are unable to assume that Sir James Ross will reach Banks Land. Sir Edward Parry was unable to reach it, and merely viewed it from a distance; much less are we able to assume that the gallant officer will find a high road to Victoria Land, which is altogether a *terra incognita.*

The main point, then, for consideration is, the effort of Sir James Ross along the western land of North Somerset from his station in Barrow Strait; for it is that alone which can supersede the necessity for the plan I have proposed. It is not in Sir John Richardson's power, it must be borne in mind, to search the western land of North Somerset. Mr. Thomas Simpson, who surveyed the arctic coast comprised between the Coppermine and Castor and Pollux Rivers, has set that question at rest, —and he is the only authority upon the subject. " A further exploration," remarks Mr. Simpson from the most eastern limit of his journey, " would necessarily demand the " whole time and energies of another Ex- " pedition, having some point of retreat " much nearer to the scene of operations " than the Great Bear Lake[5];"—and Great Bear Lake is to be the retreat of Sir John Richardson.

What retreat, my Lord, could Mr. Simpson have meant but Great Slave Lake—the retreat of the land party in search of Sir John Ross?—and what other road to the

[5] "Narrative of Discovery on the North Coast of " America," by Mr. T. Simpson, 8vo. p. 377.

unexplored ground, the western land of North Somerset, could that traveller have had in his mind but the Great Fish River—that stream which I have pointed out to your Lordship as the ice-free and the high road to the land where the lost Expedition is likely to be found—to the boundary of that "Passage," which, for three and a half centuries, we have in vain been endeavouring to reach in ships?

It is generally admitted that Mr. Thomas Simpson was "no common man." Besides, he was assisted in his memorable journey by McKay, Sinclair, and Taylor—the bowsman, the steersman, and the chief middleman and despatch-carrier to the land journey in search of Sir John Ross;—men who, I can assure your Lordship after three years' experience of their service, were of no common stamp. Sir John Richardson cannot have such assistance—death has done its work!

If Mr. Simpson, in the youth of his life, with such assistance, could not make a greater distance from his winter-quarters on the Great Bear Lake than Castor and Pollux River,—and if that great man, at that distance from his winter retreat, considered that "any further fool-hardy per-"severance could only lead to the loss of "the whole party[6],"—can more be expected of Sir John Richardson at his period of life? It is physically impossible, therefore, that Sir John Richardson can occupy the field which I have proposed for myself. This is evidently, then, the question of importance in relation to my proposal;—Do the attempts of Sir James Ross to search the western land of North Somerset in boats, from his station on the southern shores of Barrow Strait, render that proposal unnecessary?

Here, my Lord, the facts will speak for themselves. 1st. Barrow Strait was ice-bound in 1832;—it may be ice-bound in 1848. 2nd. Sir James Ross is using the same means to relieve Sir John Franklin which has led the gallant officer into difficulty; the relief party themselves may, therefore, become a party in distress. 3rd. The land that is made on the south shore of

[6] Despatch of Mr. T. Simpson to the Hudson's Bay Company, published in *The Times* of April 18, 1840.

Barrow Strait will be of doubtful character, —the natural consequence of discovery in ships; the searching parties at the end of the summer,—with the close of which every soul of the lost Expedition will have perished, may find they have been coasting an island many miles distant from the western land of North Somerset, or navigating a deep bay, as Kotzebue navigated the sound named after him.

These difficulties have so repeatedly occurred, that your Lordship will find ample facts in the narratives of the several Polar Sea Expeditions to testify to the truthfulness of these remarks. The plan which I have proposed to your Lordship is to reach the Polar Sea across the continent of America, —and thus to proceed from land known to be continent, where every footstep is sure. If that plan be laid aside, the lives of our lost countrymen will depend upon a single throw in the face of almost certain failure— if the difficulty in which the lost Expedition is involved is the same which (not to go farther back than 1818) has driven away every officer, including even Parry himself, who has made the attempt. Further, if that plan should ultimately prove to have been the right one, it will be a source of regret that your Lordship will feel most intensely. It is impossible Lord Stanley can help regretting he did not set in motion the service I proposed to him in conjunction with that of Sir John Franklin,—although in that case it was simply a question of science, and the awful calamity, which has in all probability befallen the lost Expedition, was merely a supposition on my part. How much greater, then, will be the regret of your Lordship if, at the expiration of two years, it shall be proved that my supposition, regarding the relief to Sir John Franklin,—which is a question, not of science, but of life and death on a great scale,—was equally well founded?

To sum up in a few words.—The Board of Admiralty, by their "effort," virtually declare that the lost Expedition cannot be relieved unless the "Passage" be discovered; we must first discover the "Passage," and then seek out the lost Expedition. To this declaration, my Lord, I cannot assent; for by following out my plan, I can search all that is known of the western land of North Somerset,—and be sure that every inch of discovery beyond it is so much good work for the safety of the lost Expedition and for the furtherance of geographical and natural historical knowledge. In addition, I can trace Victoria Land north with the same results,—and yet not discover the North-west Passage, nor incur the risk of any extraordinary difficulty; while Sir James Ross, before he gets a single footing on either of these lands, must have solved the problem which has baffled all our ingenuity in ships for a period of three and a half centuries.

I trust, therefore, your Lordship will give full consideration to my offer of service in search of the lost Expedition. It is a service in which I can act independently of Sir James Ross, and independently of Sir John Richardson; and Sir James Ross and Sir John Richardson, it is already arranged, are to act independently of each other. Sir James Ross's knowledge of Barrow Strait—Sir John Richardson's knowledge of the Mackenzie and the Coppermine Rivers—and my knowledge of the Great Fish River and its estuary, will be so many guarantees that the work to be done will be done well; and this state of independence will insure a large amount of effort, even though it were merely in a spirit of emulation.

Your Lordship, as Lord Howick, gave the Expedition in search of Sir John Ross your valuable assistance, and if you will but give the same encouraging assistance to the effort in search of Sir John Franklin, and fill up the blank which the Board of Admiralty have left, the country will have reason to be satisfied that all that could be done was done for the safety of the one hundred and thirty-eight gallant men, who nobly volunteered their services in spite of the danger and difficulties they were certain to meet with, merely because they were asked to do so.

I have, &c.

RICHARD KING.

Again.

To The Right Hon. Earl Grey.

17, *Savile Row, Dec.* 16, 1847.

MY LORD,—I have the honour to acknowledge the receipt of Mr. Hawes's letter of the 8th instant. Mr. Hawes states, "I am desired by Earl Grey to acknowledge "the receipt of your letter of the 25th "ultimo, in which you solicit employment "in connection with the Expedition which "you state is about to be sent out in search "of Sir John Franklin; and I am to acquaint "you in answer that it does not fall within "his Lordship's province, as Secretary of "State for the Colonies, to confer appoint- "ments of this nature, but that you should "address any application you may desire to "make upon the subject to the Lords Com- "missioners of the Admiralty."

I can scarcely express to your Lordship the deep sorrow which I felt at receiving such an answer—especially at the eleventh hour; for your Lordship has been in possession of my views of the position of Sir John Franklin's Arctic Expedition, and the means of affording it relief, since last June; and, in February, the service that I have proposed, if it be adopted, must be in progress.

Your Lordship is labouring altogether under a misconception of the views expressed in that letter. I am not "soliciting em-"ployment in connection with the Expe-"dition which is about to be sent out in "search of Sir John Franklin." I am endeavouring to induce your Lordship to take measures which I believe to be necessary for saving the lives of one hundred and thirty-eight of our fellow-creatures. So far from soliciting employment—so far from desiring to continue a Polar traveller,—I have long since ceased to be a candidate for such an office, my services in search of Sir John Ross not having been even acknowledged by the Colonial and Admiralty Boards; and it is only for the sake of humanity that I am induced to come forward again in such a character. It would not be in your Lordship's power to make good the loss which I should sustain in going in search of Sir John Franklin—a loss which cannot be measured by a money standard; and, as for employment, I should have to resign five appointments of honour and emolument which I hold, together with my professional practice.

It is not for me to question your Lordship's province as Secretary of State for the Colonies, but it is for me to consider whether I "should address any application I may "desire to make upon the subject" to the Admiralty Board. The manner in which that Board met my offer to administer medical relief to the suffering crew of the steamer Éclair, and the suppression of my name in the return made to the House of Commons, on the motion of Admiral Dundas, and ordered to be printed 13th March 1846, of officers and men who volunteered to serve on that occasion, and the hostile feeling which has prevailed at the Admiralty against my views on Arctic discoveries—all of which have now been proved to be correct,—are sufficient reasons for my not offering my services to that Board. Some changes must have taken place if it does not fall within your Lordship's province to originate expeditions of the nature which I have suggested, for Earl Bathurst despatched the overland journeys in command of Sir John Franklin, and Viscount Goderich the Expedition in search of Sir John Ross,—so that all the Polar land journeys have emanated from the Colonial Board.

For the sake of our suffering fellow-countrymen, whose miseries and hardships I can perhaps above most men conceive and appreciate, I deeply regret your Lordship's determination.

I have, &c.

RICHARD KING.

I did not long consider over the course I should pursue, but addressed the Board of Admiralty in these words:—

17, *Savile Row, February* 1848.

My Lords,—" The old route of Parry,
" through Lancaster Sound and Barrow
" Strait, as far as to the last land on its
" southern shore, and thence in a direct

" line to Behring Straits, is the route " ordered to be pursued by Franklin[7]."

The gallant officer has thus been despatched to push his adventurous way between Melville Island and Banks Land, which Sir Edward Parry attempted for two years unsuccessfully. After much toil and hardship, and the best consideration that great man could give to the subject, he recorded, at the moment of retreat, in indelible characters these impressive thoughts; —" We have been lying near our present " station, with an easterly wind blowing " fresh, for thirty-six hours together, and " although this was considerably off the " land, the ice had not during the whole " of that time moved a single yard from " the shore, affording a proof that there " was no space in which the ice was at " liberty to move to the westward. The " navigation of this part of the Polar Sea " is only to be performed by watching the " occasional openings between the ice and " the shore, and that, therefore, a con- " tinuity of land is essential for this

[7] Barrow's Arctic Voyages, p. 11.

" purpose; such a continuity of land, which " was here about to fail us, must necessarily " be furnished by the northern coast of " America, in whatsoever latitude it may " be found." Assuming, therefore, Sir John Franklin has been arrested between Melville Island and Banks Land, where Sir Edward Parry was arrested by difficulties which he considered insurmountable, and he has followed the advice of that gallant officer, and made for the continent of America, he will have turned the prows of his vessels South and West, according as Banks Land trends for Victoria or Wollaston Lands. It is here, therefore, we may expect to find the expedition wrecked, whence they will make in their boats for the western land of North Somerset, if that land should not be too far distant.

In order to save the party from the ordeal of a fourth winter, when starvation must be their lot, I propose to undertake the boldest journey that has ever been attempted in the northern regions of America, one which is justifiable only from the circumstances. I propose to attempt to reach the western land of North Somerset, or the eastern portion of Victoria Land, as may be deemed advisable, by the close of the approaching summer; to accomplish, in fact, in one summer that which has not been done under two.

I rest my hope of success in the performance of this Herculean task upon the fact that I possess an intimate knowledge of the country and the people through which I shall have to pass, the health to stand the rigour of the climate, and the strength to undergo the fatigue of mind and body to which I must be subjected. It is because I have these requisites, which I conscientiously believe are not to be found in another, that I hope to effect my purpose. A glance at the map of North America, directed to Behring Strait in the Pacific, Barrow Strait in the Atlantic, and the land of North Somerset between them, will make it apparent that, to render assistance to a party situated on that coast, there are two ways by sea and one by land. Of the two sea-ways, the route by the Pacific is altogether out of the question; it is an idea of by-gone days; while that by the Atlantic is so doubtful of success, that it is merely necessary, to put this assistance aside as far from certain, to mention that Sir John Ross found Barrow Strait closed in the summer of 1832. To a land journey, then, alone we can look for success; for the failure of a land journey would be the exception to the rule, while the failure of a sea expedition would be the rule itself. To the western land of North Somerset, where Sir John Franklin is likely to be found, the Great Fish River is the direct and only route; and although the approach to it is through a country too poor and too difficult of access to admit of the transport of provisions, it may be made the medium of communication between the lost expedition and the civilised world, and guides be thus placed at their disposal to convey them to the hunting grounds of the Indians. Without such guides it is impossible they can reach these hunting grounds. It was by the Great Fish River I reached the Polar Sea while acting as second officer in search of Sir John Ross. I feel it my duty therefore, as one of two officers so peculiarly circumstanced, to place my views on record as an earnest of my sincerity. Even if it should be determined to try and force provision vessels through Barrow Strait, and scour the vicinity in boats for the lost expedition, and should it succeed, it will be satisfactory to know such a mission as I have proposed was adopted; while if these attempts should fail, and the service under consideration be put aside, it will be a source of regret that not only the nation at large will feel, but the whole civilised world. When this regret is felt, and every soul has perished, such a mission as I have proposed will be urged again and again for adoption; for it is impossible that the country will rest satisfied until a search be made for the remains of the lost expedition by a person in whom the country has confidence.

The fact that all lands which have a western aspect are generally ice free, which I dwelt largely upon when Sir John Franklin sailed, must have had weight with the gallant officer; he will, therefore, on finding himself in a serious difficulty, while pushing along the eastern side of Victoria Land, at once fall upon the Western Land of North Somerset, as a refuge ground, if he have the opportunity. The effort by Behring Strait and Banks Land is praiseworthy in attempt, but forlorn in hope. In the former effort, it is assumed that Sir John Franklin has made the " Passage, and that his arrest is between the Mackenzie River and Icy Cape; in the latter, that Sir James Ross will reach Banks Land, and trace its continuity to Victoria and Wollaston Land, and thus make the " Passage." First, we have no reason to believe Sir John Franklin and Sir James Ross will be more fortunate than their predecessors, and we cannot trust to their success. Secondly, we are unable to assume that Sir James Ross will reach Banks Land; Sir Edward Parry was unable to reach it, and only viewed it from a distance; much less are we able to assume that the gallant officer will find a high road to Victoria Land, which is altogether a *terra incognita.*

The main point, then, for consideration,

is the effort of Sir James Ross along the Western Land of North Somerset, from his station in Barrow Strait; for it is that alone which can supersede the plan I have proposed. It is not in Sir John Richardson's power, it must be borne in mind, to search the Western Land of North Somerset. Mr. T. Simpson, who surveyed the Arctic coast comprised between the Coppermine and Castor and Pollux Rivers, has set that question at rest, and he is the only authority upon the subject. "A further "exploration," remarks Mr. Simpson, from the most eastern limit of his journey, "would necessarily demand the whole time "and energies of another expedition, having "some point of retreat much nearer to the "scene of operations than Great Bear "Lake[8]," and Great Bear Lake is the retreat of Sir John Richardson.

What retreat could Mr. Simpson have meant but Great Slave Lake, the retreat of the land party in search of Sir John Ross, to which party I was second officer,

[8] Simpson's Narrative of a Journey to the Arctic Ocean, p. 377.

but acting first officer for two-thirds of the period of its activity? and what other road to the unexplored ground, the Western Land of North Somerset, could that traveller have meant than the Great Fish River, that magnificent stream which I have pointed out as the ice-free and high-road to the land where the lost expedition is likely to be found, to the boundary of that "Passage" which for three-and-a-half centuries we have in vain been endeavouring to reach in ships?

If Mr. Simpson, in the youth of his life, with three of my best and most faithful crew down the Great Fish River in his service, could not make a greater distance from his winter quarters on the Great Bear Lake than Castor and Pollux River, and if that great man at that distance from his winter retreat "considered that any further "fool-hardy perseverance could only lead to "the loss of the whole party," can more be expected of Sir John Richardson at his period of life? It is physically impossible Sir John Richardson can occupy the field I am proposing for myself.

This, then, is evidently the question of importance. Does the attempt of Sir James Ross to search the Western Land of North Somerset in boats from his station in Barrow Strait render that proposal unnecessary? Here facts speak for themselves. 1st, Barrow Strait was ice-bound in 1832; it may be ice-bound in 1848. 2nd, Sir James Ross is using the same means to relieve Sir John Franklin which led that gallant officer into difficulty,—the relief party may, therefore, become a party in distress. 3rd, The land that is made on the South shore of Barrow Strait will be of doubtful character, the natural consequence of discovery in ships; the searching parties at the end of the summer may, therefore, find they have been coasting an island many miles distant from the Western Land of North Somerset, or navigating a deep bay, as Kotzebue navigated the sound named after him, and as Sir John Franklin navigated the sea called Melville Sound; these difficulties have so repeatedly occurred, that ample facts will be found in the narratives of the several

Polar Sea Expeditions to testify to the truthfulness of the remarks. The plan I have proposed is to reach the Polar Sea across the Continent of America, and thus to proceed from land known to be continent, where each footstep is sure. If that plan be laid aside, the lives of our lost countrymen will depend upon a single throw, in the face of almost certain failure, if the difficulty in which the lost expedition is involved is the same which (not to go farther back than 1818,) has driven away every officer, including even Parry himself, who has made the attempt.

It is because Earl Grey informs me "it "does not fall within his Lordship's "province, as Secretary of State for the "Colonies, to confer appointments of this "nature, but that I should address any "application I may desire to make upon "the subject to the Lords Commissioners "of the Admiralty," that I am induced to offer to your Lordships to go in search of Sir John Franklin by the Great Fish River.

I am, &c.

RICHARD KING.

Again.

17, *Savile Row, 3rd March,* '48.

SIR,—I beg to remind you that, on the 16th ultimo, I volunteered my services to the Lords Commissioners of the Admiralty to proceed to the Western Land of North Somerset, by the Great Fish River, in search of Sir John Franklin.

The 15th instant is the latest period I should feel justified in starting upon this expedition; and as I am not aware of having written anything to cause their Lordships to withhold a reply, and as I have to make arrangements to vacate my appointments as Physician to the London and Continental Fire and Life Office, Physician to the Blenheim Street Dispensary, Honorary Secretary of the Ethnological Society, and Assistant Secretary of the Statistical Society, I need scarcely state that it is important I should have very early information of their Lordships' decision.

I shall only be too happy to explain my plan to you by chart, as I did to Mr. Hawes, when in official communication with Earl Grey: and, in conclusion, I beg to say that I am induced thus to urge it upon the consideration of the Board, from the fact that I have given it the most mature and deliberate consideration, and that I am convinced it will eventually prove to be the only effectual one for discovering the lost expedition.

I have, &c.

RICHARD KING.

Henry George Ward, Esq.

Admiralty, 3rd March, 1848.

Sir,—In reply to your letters of this day's date, and of the 16th ultimo, offering your services to proceed to the Western Land of North Somerset by the Great Fish River, in search of the Expedition under Captain Sir John Franklin, I am commanded by my Lords Commissioners of the Admiralty to acquaint you that they have no intention of altering their present arrangements, or of making any others, that will require your assistance, or force you to make the sacrifices which you appear to contemplate.

I am, Sir,

Your most obedient, humble Servant,

H. G. WARD.

To Dr. King, 17, Savile Row.

With the view of inducing any of the whaling ships, which resort to Davis Strait and Baffin Bay, to make effort in search of the expedition under the command of Sir John Franklin, Lady Franklin, on the 20th March, 1848, offered £.1000 to any of the whaling ships finding the above expedition in distress, and an additional sum of £.1000 to any ship which should, at an early period of the season, make extraordinary exertions for the above object, and, if required, bring Sir John Franklin and his party to England.

I thought proper in consequence to address Lady Franklin as follows;—

17, *Savile Row*, 29*th March*, 1848.

MADAM,—I have just read your offer to the Northern Whalers for the relief of Sir John Franklin, and as you may perhaps be aware I have taken a great interest in the subject, I hope you will excuse my saying that your offer is altogether out of the question. It will not be accepted either for its value or for its soundness of judgment. You have been very ill-advised.

If you had offered £.1000 for an expedition down the Great Fish River, and another £.1000 for an expedition down the Coppermine River, a large portion of the coast line might have been searched in the summer of 1849[9], a year in advance of Sir John Richardson's Land Journey; and if not altogether in advance of Sir James Ross' Sea Expedition, at all events about the same time the gallant officer will be *en route*; for as a searching party he leads a " forlorn hope." And if such an offer had been made a month only ago, the whole coast line from the Coppermine River to the

[9] The Franklin Expedition was alive in 1850.

Western Land of North Somerset might have been searched by the close of this summer (1848).

I have the honour to be, &c.,

RICHARD KING.

Lady Franklin.

Although I laboured in favour of a land journey by the Great Fish River altogether in vain, an amount of effort, in search of The Franklin Expedition, was made by the Admiralty, highly creditable to them but for the manifest incompleteness of that effort,—the search which I proposed between the Coppermine and Great Fish Rivers not forming a part. The search comprised three distinct expeditions. At the same time that Sir James Ross was dispatched by the Atlantic to penetrate through Lancaster Sound, into the Polar Sea from East to West, Captain Moore was sent by the Pacific, through Behring Strait, to plough that sea of ice in the opposite direction;—and Sir John Richardson was charged with a land journey to search the polar coast between the Mackenzie and the Coppermine Rivers.

As to results, it would not be necessary to allude to the effort through Behring Strait, were it not to bring into notice the exertions of an officer who has earned for himself in polar research, a name for talent and enterprise that calls forth our highest admiration. I allude to Lieut. Bedford Pim, R.N.[10], who learnt in this barren field his first lesson in polar discovery.

The effort of Sir John Richardson, though ably conducted as far as it went, was only in part carried out, and thus yielded no fruit. Nor could, in fact, Sir John Richardson be expected to gather fruit when he had a bias, " with respect to the Great Fish " River. He did not think, under any " circumstances, Sir John Franklin would " attempt that route."

I wish I could say one kind word for Sir James Ross, for it was to his search, following as it did in the wake of The Franklin Expedition, that the nation, nay, the whole world, was looking for success.

[10] This gallant officer is now in the Baltic, in command of the Magpie gun-boat.

I cannot. If ever one man sacrificed another, Sir James Ross sacrificed Sir John Franklin, and not only Sir John Franklin, but one hundred and thirty-seven noble hearts with him. Sir James Ross, like Sir John Richardson, started with a bias against The Franklin Expedition being at the Great Fish River. "I cannot conceive," he says, "any position in which they could "be placed from which they would make "for the Great Fish River;—they would "assuredly endeavour to reach Lancaster "Sound[11]." This is stated in a letter addressed to the Admiralty against my views of the position of The Franklin Expedition, and of the mode of affording it relief; denying in vulgar language the whole of my premises, and, thus ill-conditioned, Sir James Ross rushed headlong upon a shoal and wrecked himself at once and for ever.

Addressing Lord Auckland as First Lord of the Admiralty, Sir John Ross, the uncle, says, on the eve of the departure of Sir James Ross, the nephew, "he can have no

[11] Return to an address of the House of Commons, ordered to be printed 13th April, 1848.

" intention of searching for Sir John " Franklin, his object is the 'Passage,' by " surveying the western coast of North " Somerset." His Lordship replied, " I " shall take care of that and order him to " the north shore of Barrow Strait, and his " second in command to the western shore " of North Somerset. Lord Auckland in " his orders was as good as his word. " Nevertheless Sir James Ross, as I had " anticipated, found an excuse to occupy " the ground laid out for his second in " command (from whom he kept the " orders secret), in direct violation of the " Admiralty instructions[12]

" By an extraordinary amount of delay, " hitherto unaccounted for, he lost the " chances offered by his first season, and " in his second season his puny efforts, " compared with the necessities of the case, " are too contemptible to invite criticism, " and but for the stern and tragic asso- " ciations of the expedition, might provoke " ridicule. It is melancholy to contemplate

[12] " Narrative, &c., of Sir John Ross," Longman, London, 1855, p. 32.

" this most deplorable beginning of a series " of unsuccessful expeditions which have " cost the country the expenditure of a " vast treasure, and uniformly led to " failure and disappointment. If we had " nothing more to complain of than the " mere sacrifice of treasure, it would " be a matter of little consequence, but " when it is recollected, as subsequent " discoveries have shewn, that at least a " portion, and an important one, of the " party of Sir John Franklin was wandering " within 150 miles of Sir James Ross' " Expedition, on the brink of famine, and " probably worn out by disease, calamity, " and fatigue, it is impossible not to regard " this parsimonious exercise of effort and " fatal loss of time as one of the greatest " calamities that has ever befallen our " happy country[13].

On the return of Sir James Ross the sympathies of the whole world were aroused to the fate of The Franklin Expedition. A weak Government was no longer to be trusted "with the lives of men who

[13] "Narrative, &c., of Sir John Ross," Longman, London, 1855, p. 32.

" nobly perilled everything in the cause of " national—nay, of universal progress and " knowledge;—of men who evinced in this " and other expeditions the most dauntless " bravery that any men can evince[14]." Thus three private expeditions were dispatched in command of Sir John Ross and Commander Forsyth, on behalf of the British public; and Lieutenant De Haven, on behalf of the citizens of the United States.

And because of this voluntary effort the Admiralty, parsimonious at first to a fault, ran riot, and dispatched a whole fleet; not, however, upon a basis of action, but all in one direction, in the very opposite direction to that clearly pointed out by the recent search;—in the direction, Sir John Franklin, if he had obeyed orders, was not to be found. The Investigator, Captain M'Clure, and the Enterprise, Captain Collinson, were dispatched by Behring Strait. The Resolute, Captain Austin; the Assistance, Captain Ommanney; the Intrepid, Lieutenant Cator; the Pioneer, Lieutenant Osborne; the Lady Franklin, Captain Penny; and the Sophia,

[14] *Athenæum.*

Captain Stewart; were dispatched by Barrow Strait. Again the Polar coast line between the Coppermine and the Great Fish Rivers was left out of the search; for the second time, therefore, I addressed the Secretary of the Admiralty,—

17, *Savile Row*, 18*th February*, 1850.

Sir,—The period having arrived when a search may be made for The Franklin Expedition by an overland journey across the continent of America, I am anxious to refer my Lords Commissioners of the Admiralty, for reconsideration, to my plan, dated February 1848, and published in a return to an address of the honourable the House of Commons of the 21st of March following.

The opinion of Captain Sir Edward Parry, published in that return, was highly favourable to the position I assigned to the lost expedition,—the Western Land of North Somerset, and to the mode in which I proposed to reach it (by the Great Fish River); but the gallant and intrepid officer, "agree-" ing thus far, was compelled to differ with

" me as to the *readiest mode* of reaching
" that coast, because he felt satisfied that
" with the resources of the expedition then
" equipping under Sir James Ross, the
" energy, skill, and intelligence of that
" officer would render it a matter of no
" very difficult enterprise to examine the
" coast in question with his ships, boats, or
" travelling parties."

In the plan to which I am now asking their Lordships' reconsideration, this question, which I premised might be raised, is thus argued by me :—" Does the attempt of
" Sir James Ross to reach the Western Land
" of North Somerset in boats from his
" station in Barrow Strait, render that pro-
" posal unnecessary? (to reach the Western
" Land of North Somerset by the Great
" Fish River.) Here facts will speak for
" themselves: 1st, Barrow Strait was
" ice-bound in 1832; it may therefore *be*
" *ice-bound in* 1848. 2nd, Sir James Ross is
" using the same means to relieve Sir John
" Franklin which led the gallant officer
" into difficulty; the relief party may,
" therefore, become a party in distress.

" 3rd, The land that is made on the south
" shore of Barrow Strait will be of doubtful
" character, the natural consequence of
" discovery in ships; the searching party,
" at the end of the summer, may therefore
" find they have been coasting an island
" many miles distant from the Western Land
" of North Somerset, or navigating a deep
" bay, as Kotzebue navigated the sound
" named after him, and as Sir John Franklin
" navigated the sea called Melville Sound.

" The plan which I have proposed is, to
" reach the Polar Sea across the Continent
" of America, and thus to proceed from
" land known to be continent, where each
" footstep is sure. If that plan be laid
" aside, the lives of our lost countrymen
" will *depend upon a single throw*, in the
" face of almost certain failure."

This only difference between Sir Edward Parry and myself, in 1848, is now, in 1850, at an end. Barrow Strait was ice-bound. The *single throw* fell far short of its mark. Captain Sir James Ross failed in affording the least succour to the lost Expedition and I am thus spared the painful necessity of replying to the gallant officer's remarks expressed to their Lordships, in no measured terms, upon that plan which, in fact, Sir Edward Parry has done for me,—the plan of one who learnt his lesson in active discovery in an overland journey in search of the gallant officer when the whole civilised world was as anxious for his fate as it is now for the gallant Sir John Franklin.

All that has been done by way of search since February 1848, tends to draw attention closer and closer to the West Land of North Somerset as the position of Sir John Franklin, and to the Great Fish River as the high road to reach it. Such a plan as I proposed to their Lordships in 1848 is consequently of the utmost importance. It would be the happiest moment of my life—(and my delight at being selected from a long list of volunteers for the relief of Sir John Ross was very great)—if their Lordships would allow me to go by my old route, the Great Fish River, to attempt to save human life a second time on the shores of the Polar Sea. What I did in search of

Sir John Ross is the best earnest of what I could do in search of Sir John Franklin.

That the route by the Great Fish River will sooner or later be undertaken, in search of Sir John Franklin, I have no doubt That high road to the land where I have all along maintained Sir John Franklin would be found, and in which opinion I am now associated with many others, including Sir Edward Parry himself, cannot much longer be neglected. For some time past it has been the cry, even in the highest official quarters, that the Government will not again attempt the discovery of the North-west Passage, and the fate of Sir John Franklin is invariably referred to as an example of the fruitlessness of such an attempt.

The fruitlessness of Sir John Franklin s attempt ought not to discredit the service in which he is engaged, but rather to awaken us to the grievous error committed in the instructions which he received, and upon which it is impossible to look back without the most painful feelings.

The gallant officer is, in fact, instructed to lead a "forlorn hope." The discovery of the North-west Passage is the certain result of so overwhelming a catastrophe.

In the absence of authentic information of the fate of the gallant band of adventurers, the *terra incognita* of the North Coast of North America will not only be traced, but minutely surveyed, and the solution of the problem of centuries will engage the marked attention of the House of Commons and the Legislative Assemblies in other parts of the world. The problem is very safe in their hands, so safe, indeed, that I venture to assert five years will not elapse before it is solved[15].

I may be allowed to state, in urging my claims to conduct an expedition down the Great Fish River, whenever such a service is determined by their Lordships, that, in addition to my intimate knowledge of that stream, I persisted, single-handed, for several years prior to the discovery, in maintaining the existence of three most

[15] The North-West Passage problem was solved by Captain M'Clure in 1853

important features of the Northern Coast of North America,—the Peninsula of North Somerset,—the Great Bay of Simpson,—and Cape Britannia, all of which are now established geographical facts.

I have the honour to be, &c.,

RICHARD KING

Admiralty, 28*th February*, 1850.

SIR,—Having laid before my Lords Commissioners of the Admiralty your letter of the 18th instant, stating your plan for affording relief to the Expedition under Sir John Franklin, I am commanded by their Lordships to thank you for the same, but I am to acquaint you that they must decline the offer of your services.

I am, SIR,

Your very humble Servant,

W. B. HAMILTON.

DR. KING, 17, Savile Row.

And here I had to take my stand.

The *Athenæum*, ever ready to lend a helping hand to The Franklin Expedition, sent forth to the fleet of explorers in the Arctic sea this touching appeal:—

"There is something intensely in-
"teresting in the picture of those dreary
"seas, amid whose strange and unspeak-
"able solitudes our lost countrymen have
"been somewhere imprisoned for so many
"years, swarming with the human life that
"is risked to set them free. No hunt was
"ever so exciting—so full of a wild
"grandeur and a profound pathos—as that
"which has just aroused the Arctic echoes;
"that wherein their brothers and com-
"panions have been beating for the track
"by which they may rescue the lost
"mariners from the icy grasp of the genius
"of the North. Fancy these men in their
"adamantine prison, wherever it may be—
"chained up by the Polar spirit, whom
"they had dared—lingering through years
"of cold and darkness on the stunted ration
"that scarcely feeds the blood, and the
"feeble hope that scarcely sustains the
"heart,—and then imagine the rush of
"emotions to greet the first cry from that

" wild hunting ground which shall reach " their ears! Through many summers has " that cry been listened for, no doubt. " Something like an expectation of the " rescue, which it should announce, has " revived with each returning season of " comparative light, to die of its own " baffled intensity as long as the dark " months once more settled down upon " their dreary prison house."

The results of the *fleet of vessels* sent forth in 1850 are briefly told. Commander Forsyth and Lieutenant De Haven were altogether unsuccessful; they failed in establishing even a wintering, and merely made the voyage to the Polar Sea and back. Sir John Ross secured his wintering, and that is all. Captain Austen, however, on on his arrival at winter quarters in Barrow Strait, set vigorously to work, and planned a winter search for The Franklin Expedition upon a scale equal to the emergency, upon a system of organization which reflects the highest credit upon this distinguished officer, now actively engaged as Captain-Superintendent of Deptford Dockyard. Both in conception and execution the

Austen Winter Search for The Franklin Expedition will ever form an epoch in Polar History. Travelling parties in sledges over the ice, searched far and wide along the shores of Barrow Strait and Wellington Channel, and as far West as Melville Island; but not a trace of the lost adventurers was discovered. The Parry Sandstone, the Post Office of the North Pole, was examined but no record found. The Franklin Expedition had not been there.

This is not the place to give the natural historical knowledge brought to light by the gallant officers charged with carrying out Captain Austen's noble errand of mercy. The future historian of the North Pole will have that pleasure. He will not fail to recognise in Mr. Bradford, and Lieutenants Osborne and M'Clintock, men of unbounded energy and resource. That The Franklin Expedition "died of official pigheadedness and Admiralty neglect[15]" was not their fault.

Captain Penny has the merit of having discovered Sir John Franklin's first wintering in 1846-7, at Beechy Island. He

[15] *Atlas*, 28th October, 1854.

first found the trail, but "what of the "weary feet that made it? We cannot "hear of this sudden discovery of traces "of the vanished crews as living men, "without a wish which comes like a pang "that it had been two years ago, or even "last year. It makes the heart sore to "think how close relief may have been "to their hiding-place in former years, "when it turned away. There is scarcely "reason to doubt that, had the present "circumstances of the search occurred two "years ago—last year perhaps—its wan-"derers would have been restored. "Another year makes a frightful difference "in the odds; and we do not think the "public will ever feel satisfied with what "has been done in this matter, if the oracle "so long questioned, and silent so long, "shall speak at last, and the answer shall "be 'It is too late[16].'"

It is difficult, at this stage of the proceedings to understand how the Admiralty could have possibly gone wrong. Captain Austen's thorough but fruitless exploration from Barrow Strait to Melville Island, in the

[16] *Athenæum.*

wake of The Franklin Expedition, had *closed the search* in that direction, and Sir James Ross's perversion of his errand of mercy had *left open the search* in the direction of the Great Fish River. But the Admiralty, manifestly the most inefficient of all the Government Boards, were determined to go wrong; and, goaded by an outward pressure, for the English House of Commons and the United States Congress had now taken up the subject, called into existence an Arctic Council to give a colouring to their own acts and deeds; the men appointed, with one exception, having already pledged themselves to particular views.

The Arctic Council comprised—

Sir Francis Beaufort.	Colonel Sabine.
Sir Edward Parry.	Captain Hamilton.
Sir John Richardson.	Captain Bird.
Sir James Ross.	Captain Beechy.
Sir George Back.	Mr. Barrow.

Of the Council of ten, to whom the Admiralty, in their extremity, had committed the fate of the Franklin Expedition, Captain Hamilton, Captain Bird, and Mr. Barrow have not recorded their opinions.

Sir Francis Beaufort,—" If they had

" reached much to the South of Banks Land " they would surely have communicated " with the tribes on the Mackenzie. The " general conclusion is, that they are locked " up in the Archipelago, to the West of " Melville Island."

Sir Edward Parry,—" We know Franklin " did intend, if he could not get westward, " to go up Wellington Channel. We have " it from his own lips. My belief is still, " that, after the first winter, he did go up."

Sir John Richardson,—" With respect to " the Great Fish River, he did not think, " under any circumstances, Sir John " Franklin would attempt that route."

Sir James Ross,—" I cannot conceive any " position in which The Franklin Expedition " could be placed, from which they would " make for the Great Fish River;—they " would assuredly endeavour to reach " Lancaster Sound."

Sir George Back, addressing the Secretary of the Admiralty,—" You will be pleased, " Sir, to impress on my Lords Commissioners " that, I *wholly* reject *all* and *every* idea of " *any* attempts on the part of Sir John " Franklin to send boats or detachments "over the ice to *any* point of the mainland "in the vicinity of the Great Fish River."

Colonel Sabine "conceived that the crews "may have been at length obliged to quit "their ships and attempt a retreat, *not* "towards the continent, *because too distant*, "but to Melville Island."

Why were not Sir John Ross, Captain Austen, Captain Penny, Mr. McCormick, and myself, summoned to the Arctic Council, and why was a seat in Council permitted to Sir James Ross, and Sir George Back, seeing that they were both committed over and over again to very grave errors?

It is highly creditable to the intelligence of Captain Beechy, that he alone took a comprehensive view of the subject. The gallant officer stated in 1847, "It would "render the plan complete, if a boat could "be sent down the Great Fish River to range "the coast, to the eastward of its mouth." Again, in 1849, "I am of opinion, that "nothing should be neglected in the direc-"tion of the northern coast of America, "for it seems to me almost certain, that "Sir John Franklin has abandoned his "ships and made for the continent."

Sir Edward Parry gave a very different opinion in 1847, to that which he gave as member of the Arctic Council.

1847.	1852.
"The only plan which appears to me to hold out a reasonable prospect of success is, by making an effort to push supplies to the northern coast of America, and by the modes of travelling adopted by the Hudson Bay Company[17]."	"We know Franklin did intend, if he could not get westward, to go up Wellington Channel, we have it from his own lips. My belief is still that, after the first winter he did go up that channel[18]"

Dr. Rae took an opportunity to record his opinion, and stepped out of his way to do so. Giving a description of a journey he was about to make in the direction of the Great Fish River, he says, "I do not "mention the lost navigators, as there is "not the slightest hope of finding any "traces of them in the quarter to which I "am going[19]."

Sir John Barrow, in July 1847, says, "on the coast of North America, I should "consider any inquiry unnecessary. The

[17] Narrative of Sir John Ross, Longman, p. 47.

[18] Blue Book.

[19] *Times*, Oct. 11th, 1852.

" Hudson Bay Company have their stations " so little removed from the sea-coast, " and have so much intercourse with the " Indians and Esquimaux, and besides Sir " John Franklin must have such a painful " recollection of that coast, as to avoid it in " the first instance, and if forced on it, to " lose no time in quitting it."

If the Arctic Council *ever* made a Report, the Admiralty *never* published it; and that good man, Sir Robert Harry Inglis, was not in health to enforce it. As if to put an end to a *troublesome* service—troublesome only to the Admiralty Incapables—to a service which has given birth to *hordes* of the best sailors the world ever beheld, the Admiralty now despatched, in search of The Franklin Expedition, a fleet of four ships to follow the exact course of Captain Austen from Barrow Strait to Melville Island, with the exception of the search by Wellington Strait, left to a boat Expedition entrusted to Dr. M^c^Cormick; and placed in command Sir Edward Belcher, an officer advanced in years, who had spent a whole life in proving himself to be the very last man fitted for so honourable a service.

Sir Edward Belcher's Expedition was to form itself into two divisions; while the one proceeded to Melville Island, the other was to pass up Wellington Strait. Out of *evil* sometimes comes *good;* so it was in this instance. The Melville Island division, from a memorandum deposited in the *cache* at Melville Island, called the *Parry Sandstone*, learnt that Captain McClure was hard fixed in the ice, at a place called Mercy Bay, some distance to the westward; and that he intended to desert his ships and to divide his party—one half to proceed to the Mackenzie River and the other half to Lancaster Sound.

Fortunately there existed an officer of sufficient energy of character and power of endurance to undertake one of the boldest journeys that has ever been attempted at the season of the year it was necessary to make it, in order to spare Captain McClure the awful tragedy that awaited so desperate an attempt. Captain McClure says of this journey of Lieutenant Bedford Pim—

"All description must fall below the reality. Only imagine, if you can, a whole crew, which had to this moment no idea of any ship but their own being within the limit of these dreary regions, cut off from the world, their isolated situation (and in defiance of all exertion), a little despondent, when accidentally a strange, remarkable, and solitary figure is seen rapidly advancing, shewing gesticulations of friendship similar to those used by the Esquimaux, black as Erebus from the smoke created by cooking in his tent. My surprise—I may almost add, dismay—was great in the extreme. I paused in my advance, who or what could it be, whether a denizen of this or the other world? However, the surprise was momentary. 'I am Lieutenant Bedford Pim, late of Herald[20].' And as the apparition was thus indubitably discovered to be solid, real English flesh and blood, to rush at and seize him by the hand was the first impulsive gush of feeling. The heart was too full for the tongue to articulate, as this dark stranger communicated his errand of mercy."

The part which Sir Edward Belcher played, was just what everybody clearly anticipated; and, as getting rid of a service which they were wholly incapable of appreciating or managing, just what the Admiralty evidently wanted. Not satisfied with the destruction of all and everything

[20] The gallant officer had served in the 'Herald' in a previous expedition in search of Franklin by way of the Pacific, and, as officer of the 'Herald,' was almost the last man seen by McClure when he entered the Polar Sea. It was somewhat singular that he should be also the first man seen by him upon his being about to leave it.

he had himself in charge, he insisted, as superior officer, upon the entire destruction of all and everything the gallant officer of the second division had in charge. The Resolute and Intrepid were abandoned 27 miles South-west of Cape Cockburn; the Assistance and Pioneer 40 miles up Wellington Channel; the Investigator at Mercy Bay—in all five ships, and at a time they were most wanted.

Although Sir Edward Belcher had proved himself a worthy associate of the Admiralty, and had thus drugged 'John Bull' with his favourite hobby of three centuries to the very dregs—this unparalleled desertion of five ships[21] in thorough condition, was far too good a thing even for them. They tried him by Court Martial, and returned his sword in *solemn silence*, a lesson too refined for the organisation of the man, yet one that he will not soon forget.

Dr McCormick had the special service to trace the Wellington Channel of Barrow Strait in relation to Smith and Jones Sounds of the Atlantic, having long held the opinion

[21] This was written before the discovery of the 'Resolute,' in Davis Straits, was known.

these seas opened into the Polar Ocean. The experience he had gained in former voyages, not only to the North but to the South Pole, led this hardy and gallant officer to select for his vessel a whale boat, and for his crew six men. Clothed by day in the most simple attire, and covered by night with a felt bag, into which each crept, chrysalis-like, and a buffalo robe, and provisioned for a month with the mere *necessaries* of life, this little band embarked on the 19th of August, 1852, on their adventurous errand. Commencing at Beechy Island, of Barrow Strait, the coast line of the eastern shore of the Wellington Channel was minutely examined, and several bays and headlands named as far as the northern extremity of Baring Bay, called Point Owen, without finding a tracing of The Franklin Expedition. The journey throughout was one of great difficulty; the launching of the 'Forlorn Hope,' the name he gave to his little frail boat, over the drift ice off Lovell Point, at the very commencement of the journey, and subsequently the running it under the lee of two icebergs a-ground, to save it from foundering under a heavy sea, touchingly illustrated by woodcuts from his own pencil on the spot, clearly demonstrate his practised hand in Arctic travelling. He had the satisfaction of determining that no communication existed between Baring Bay and Jones Sound.

" In the history of physical science it is " generally admitted that, though our " highest praises may be awarded to suc- " cessful endeavour, we shall not fail to " give honour due to courageous and well- " meant exertion, which may fail in reaching " the wished-for goal. To dare peril and " death in the attempt to find a North-East " or a North-West Passage, or to penetrate " into the interior of Africa, is to establish " a claim to public respect and gratitude. " It is something even to shew that in this " or that direction no pathway is to be " found[22]."

He proposed, while still at Beechy Island, to explore Smith Sound, if Sir Edward Belcher would place at his disposal the yacht Mary, and a gutta percha boat lying useless on the spot, the crew of the Forlorn Hope having again volunteered to be his

[22] Quarterly Review for October 1845, page 108.

travelling party; a proposal, however, which the gallant Commander declined. Considering the importance of Smith Sound and that on the spot existed the means of exploring it—a vessel lying useless, a volunteer crew, an intrepid Commander, possessing indomitable perseverance, and combining the special qualifications of seamanship and medical knowledge, rarely found united—it is deeply to be regretted that Dr. McCormick was not permitted to make the survey[23].

Sir Edward Belcher passed rapidly up the Wellington Channel to an expanse of islet-covered sea, named by him Northumberland Sound, where he wintered. A sledging party in the winter visited the western division of the expedition at Melville Island. and thus Sir Edward Belcher became acquainted with the discovery of the North-West Passage.

The discovery that Jones Sound formed an outlet of the Polar Sea into the Atlantic

[23] Dr. Kane, when this was written, had not discovered Smith Sound to be the inlet into a vast Polar Sea of 3000 square miles. He had not even contemplated making the survey.

was the main feature of Sir Edward Belcher's labours.

A mere accident brought McClure to the North-West Passage; a mere accident brought the Admiralty face to face with The Franklin Expedition. Murder will out, though hidden for a time at the bottom of a well, and thus the Admiralty, to whose safe keeping all that was mortal of the gallant Franklin and his devoted followers was entrusted by this great nation, stood aghast before 138 souls, and *gave up the ghost.* Thus annihilated, they had not even the decency to dispatch an officer of known ability to bury the remains, bleaching under the canopy of heaven, on the bank of the Great Fish River, but left the Hudson Bay Company to perform this sad office; and almost the last act of Sir James Graham's political existence was, to play Great Ghost on the melancholy occasion. What a blessing has Admiral Sir Charles Napier conferred upon the nation if he has really "smashed" this ex-minister, as he says he has,—"no officer of honour and character "is safe in his hands[24]."

[24] Sir Charles Napier in "*Times*" of 12th March, 1855.

Dr. Rae's Report to the Admiralty.

"REPULSE BAY, July 19, 1854.—During my journey over the ice and snows this spring, with the view of completing the survey of the west coast of Boothia, I met with Esquimaux in Pelly Bay, from one of whom I learnt that a party of 'white men' (Kabloonans) had perished from want of food, some distance to the westward, and not far beyond a large river containing many falls and rapids. Subsequently, further particulars were received and a number of articles purchased, which places the fate of a portion, if not of all, of the then survivors of Sir John Franklin's long-lost party beyond a doubt a fate as terrible as the imagination can conceive." The substance of the information ob

Dr. Rae's Report to the Hudson Bay Company.

"YORK FACTORY, Aug. 4, 1854.—I arrived here on the 31st ult., with my small party, in excellent health, but I am sorry to say without having effected our object. At the same time, information has been obtained and articles purchased from the natives, which places the fate of a portion, if not all, the then survivors of Sir John Franklin's miserable party beyond a doubt—a fate the most deplorable—death from starvation, after having had recourse to cannibalism as a means of prolonging life. I reached my old quarters at Repulse Bay, on the 15th of August, 1853, and by the end of September, 109 deer, 1 musk ox, 54 brace of ptarmigan, and one seal had been shot, and the nets produced

tained at various times and from various sources, was as follows :—

"In the spring, four winters past (spring 1850), a party of 'white men,' amounting to about 40, were seen travelling southward over the ice and dragging a boat with them by some Esquimaux, who were killing seals near the north shore of King William Land, which is a large island. None of the party could speak the Esquimaux language intelligibly, but by signs the natives were made to understand that their ship, or ships, had been crushed by the ice, and that they were now going to where they ex pected to find deer to shoot. From the appearance of the men, all of whom except one officer looked thin, they were then supposed to be getting short of provi sions, and they pur

190 salmon. On the 31st of March 1854, my spring journey commenced, but in consequence of gales of wind, deep and soft snow, and foggy weather, we made but very little progress. We did not enter Pelly Bay until the 17th. At this place we met with Esquimaux, one of whom, on being asked if he ever saw white people, replied in the negative, but said that a large party (at least 40 persons) had perished from want of food some 10 or 12 days' journey to the westward. The substance of the information obtained at various times and from various sources was as follows :—

"In the spring four winters past (spring 1850), a party of white men, amounting to about 40, were seen travelling southward over the ice and dragging a boat with them, by some Esqui-

chased a small seal from the natives. At a later date the same season, but previously to the breaking up of the ice, the bodies of some 30 persons were discovered on the continent, and five on an island near it, about a long day's journey to the N. W. of a large stream, which can be no other than Great Fish River (named by the Esquimaux *Oot-ko-hi-ca-lik*), as its description and that of the low shore in the neighbourhood of Point Ogle and Montreal Island agree exactly with that of Sir George Back. Some of the bodies had been buried (probably those of the first victims of famine); some were in a tent or tents; others under the boat, which had been turned over to form a shelter, and several lay scattered about in different directions. Of

maux, who were killing seals on the north shore of King William Land, which is a large island, named Kei ik-tak by the Esquimaux. None of the party could speak the native language intelligibly, but, by signs, the natives were made to understand that their ships or ship had been crushed in the ice, and that the whites' were now going to where they expected to find deer to shoot. From the appearance of the men, all of whom, except one officer (chief) looked thin, they were supposed to be getting short of provisions, and they purchased a small seal from the natives. At a later date of the season, but previous to the disruption of the ice, the bodies of about 30 white persons were discovered on the continent, and five on an island near it, about a

those found on the island one was supposed to have been an officer, as he had a telescope strapped over his shoulders and his double-barrel gun lay underneath him. From the mutilated state of many of the corpses and the contents of the kettles, it is evident that our wretched countrymen had been driven to the last resource—cannibalism—as a means of prolonging existence. There appeared to have been an abundant stock of ammunition, as the powder was emptied in a heap on the ground by the natives out of the kegs or cases containing it; and a quantity of ball and shot was found below high-water mark, having probably been left on the ice close to the beach. There must have been a number of watches, compasses, telescopes, guns (several double-barrelled), &c., all

long day's journey (say 35 or 40 miles) to the north-west of a large stream, which can be no other than Great Fish River, (named by the Esquimaux *Out-koo-hi-ca-lik*) as its description and that of the low shore in the neighbourhood of Point Ogle and Montreal Island agree exactly with that of Sir George Back. Some of the bodies had been buried (probably those of the first victims of famine), some were in a tent or tents, others under a boat that had been turned over to form a shelter, and several lay scattered about in different directions. Of those found on the island, one was supposed to have been an officer, as he had a telescope strapped over his shoulder and his double-barrelled gun lay underneath him. From the mutilated state of

of which appear to have been broken up, as I saw pieces of these different articles with the Esquimaux, and, together with some silver spoons and forks, purchased as many as I could get. A list of the most important of these I enclose, with a rough sketch of the crests and initials on the forks and spoons. The articles themselves shall be handed over to the Secretary of the Hon. Hudson Bay Company on my arrival in London. None of the Esquimaux with whom I conversed had seen the 'whites,' nor had they ever been at the place where the bodies were found, but had their information from those who had been there and who had seen the party when travelling.

"One silver table fork—crest, an animal's head with wings, extended above; three

many of the corpses and the contents of the kettles, it is evident that our miserable countrymen had been driven to the last resource—cannibalism—as a means of prolonging life. There appears to have been an abundant stock of ammunition, as the powder was emptied in a heap on the ground by the natives out of the kegs or cases containing it, and a quantity of ball and shot were found below high water mark, having been left on the ice close to the beach. There must have been a number of watches, telescopes, compasses, guns (several double barrelled), &c. all of which appear to have been broken up, as I saw pieces of these different articles with the Esquimaux, and together with some silver spoons and forks, purchased as many as I could obtain. A

silver table forks—crest, a bird with wings extended; one silver table spoon—crest, with initials 'F. R. M. C.' (Captain Crozier, Terror).

"One silver table spoon and one fork—crest, bird with laurel branch in mouth, motto, '*Spero meliora.*'

"One silver table spoon, one tea-spoon, and one dessert fork—crest, a fish's head looking upwards, with laurel branches on each side.

"One silver table fork—initials, 'H. D. S. G.' (Harry D. S. Goodsir, assistant-surgeon, Erebus).

"One silver table fork—initials, 'A. M'D.' (Alexander M'Donald, assistant-surgeon, Terror).

"One silver table fork—initials, 'G. A. M.' (Gillies A. Macbean, second master, Terror).

"One silver table fork—initials, 'J. T.'

"One silver dessert spoon—initials, 'J. S. P.' (John S. Peddie, surgeon, Erebus.

"One round silver plate, engraved, 'Sir John Franklin,

list of the most important of these I enclose, with a rough pen-and-ink sketch of the crests and initials on the forks and spoons. The articles themselves shall be handed over to the secretary of the H. B. Company, on my arrival in London. None of the Esquimaux with whom I conversed had seen the 'whites, nor had they ever been at the place where the dead were found, but had their information from those who had been there, and those who had seen the party when alive. From the head of Pelly Bay—which is a bay, spite of Sir F. Beaufort's opinion to the contrary, I crossed 60 miles of land in a westerly direction, traced the west shore from Castor and Pollux River to Cape Porter of Sir James Ross, and I could have got within 30 or 40 miles

K.C.B.'; a star or order, with motto, '*Nec aspera terrent*, G. R. III, MDCCCV.'

"Also a number of other articles with no marks by which they could be recog nised.

"JOHN RAE."

of Bellot Strait, but I thought it useless proceeding further, as I could not complete the whole. We arrived at Repulse Bay on the 26th May. "JOHN RAE."

That The Franklin Expedition had died to a man was not for a moment doubted, but that "our wretched countrymen had "been driven to the last resource—canni- "balism — as a means of prolonging "existence," was wholly rejected. The "Times" and the "Examiner" not only expressed their own doubt upon this part of Dr. Rae's narrative, but admitted into their columns the following letters, which I reprint because it drew forth from Dr. Rae a reply, to which I felt bound to give a rejoinder.

To the Editor of the "Times."

"Sir,—Although the opinions which I "hold on the subject of Dr. Rae's report "go something beyond what you yourself "have expressed, I trust that you will allow "this letter to appear in your paper, if it is

" only for the purpose of eliciting the senti-
" ments of others on a matter in which I
" am peculiarly interested—having had a
" brother on board Her Majesty's ship
" Terror.

" It appears to me that Dr. Rae has been
" deeply reprehensible either in not veri-
" fying the report which he received from
" the Esquimaux, or, if that was absolutely
" out of the question, in publishing the
" details of that report, resting, as they do,
" on grounds most weak and unsatisfactory.
" He had far better have kept silence alto-
" gether than have given us a story which,
" while it pains the feelings of many, must
" be very insufficient for all.

" To say nothing of the difficulties which,
" in your article of Thursday, you have
" touched upon, there are others which
" seem to me so patent that I can only
" wonder they did not occur to Dr. Rae
" himself.

" 1. Where the Esquimaux can live—
" where Dr. Rae's party could find abundant
" means—what should have prevented Sir
" John Franklin and his party from sub-
" sisting too?

" 2. When they were forced—as, no " doubt, they have been—to abandon their " ships, can any one believe that they would " have encumbered themselves with forks " and spoons and silver plates, instead of " reserving every inch of available space " for stores and articles absolutely necessary " for subsistence?

" 3. Supposing that they died by starva- " tion, is it likely that a large body of men " would have died all together? Would " they not have yielded one by one, each " struggling on as far as he could, in the " hope of either finding some store of pro- " visions or meeting some party sent out for " their rescue?

" I, Sir, for one, have long given up all " expectation of seeing my brother again in " this world. But there are many who " still cling to the hope of regaining their " relations. My own belief is, that the ships " have been abandoned and plundered by " Esquimaux. I would only persuade my- " self that I am not compelled to believe " the painful details which Dr. Rae has " most unwarrantably published. But others " believe that the crews may yet be sub-

" sisting somewhere, and, until Dr. Rae's
" report be verified, they will not part with
" their belief for anything which he has
" said. I enclose my card, and am,

" Sir, your obedient servant,

" E. J. H.

" *October* 26."

To the Editor of the " Examiner."

" Sir,—In your remarks upon Dr. Rae's
" report, you say that you limit your belief
" to the proofs of identity and death.
" Anxious for a gleam of consolation, I am
" strongly impelled to a more favourable
" conclusion. Accepting the whole story
" of the Esquimaux who were in possession
" of the property of the exploring party
" (but who, it will be observed, never saw
" them, alive or dead), we find that Franklin
" abandoned his ships, both at the same
" time, so leisurely as to carry out plate
" and a large quantity of books; that he
" travelled with a boat, but was short of
" provisions, and bought one seal—(' a small
" ' seal' amongst forty men)—yet suffered the
" natives to leave him; that his party were

" afterwards found by the Esquimaux (same
" tribe) lying dead on the ground for want
" of food (although the Esquimaux had
" kept body and soul together). That they
" had been eating dead bodies (it does not
" appear they killed any one for the purpose),
" but only to a limited extent, and not
" seriatim and methodically down to the
" last man; that they had fuel and fire, and
" were still carrying about with them their
" plate, a large quantity of books, and am-
" munition. I make no comment on a story
" so inconsistent.

" The only fact we have proof of is the
" identity of the property, which happily
" dismisses from our minds the fearful catas-
" trophe so wonderfully escaped by other
" Arctic navigators—their instantaneous
" destruction in the ice—ships and crew
" without a vestige. Dr. Rae's report
" therefore affords, I think, some ground
" for hope. Franklin may be considered
" to have had ample stock of food when he
" abandoned the ship, the stock brought
" out being actually husbanded in those
" regions where fresh provisions are met
" with, *and that great man's knowledge of*

" *his business is a security for the rest.* His
" former perilous position, referred to in
" your remarks, is not a case in point. Is
" it not the more rational conclusion that
" the Esquimaux plundered the ships, and
" that the round silver dish of Sir John
" Franklin's was found there rather than
" on his person, when wandering, Heaven
" knows whither, without food, or any
" superfluous strength to carry such gear?
" Should you think these suggestions worth
" insertion, perhaps they may lead to others
" from better-informed quarters, calculated
" to confirm the hope which I fondly
" cherish.

" *Lichfield, October* 31." " S."

To the Editor of the " Times."

" Sir,—On looking over your paper this
" morning I was deeply pained and not a
" little surprised at some remarks in a letter
" purporting to come from a brother of one
" of the officers of the unfortunate expedition
" under Sir John Franklin. The writer, in
" the first place, says 'that Dr. Rae has been
" 'deeply reprehensible for not verifying the
" 'report of the Esquimaux, and for pub-

" ' lishing his report without verification;
" ' that he should have kept silence altogether
" ' and not have excited such painful feelings
" ' in many persons on such insufficient
" ' grounds.' To have verified the reports
" which I brought home would, I believe,
" have been no difficult matter, but it could
" not possibly be done by my party in any
" other way than by passing another winter
" at Repulse Bay, and making another
" journey over the ice and snow in the spring
" of 1855. My reason for returning from
" Repulse Bay without having effected the
" survey I had contemplated was, to prevent
" the risk of more valuable lives being
" sacrificed in a useless search in portions of
" the Arctic Seas, hundreds of miles distant
" from the sad scene where so many of the
" long-lost party terminated. It is stated
" by your correspondent, ' where Esquimaux
" ' can live—where Dr. Rae's party could
" ' find abundant means — what should
" ' prevent Sir John Franklin and his party
" ' from subsisting too?' No man but one
" perfectly unacquainted with the subject
" could ask such a question. That portion
" of country near to, and on which a portion

" of Sir John Franklin's party was seen, is,
" in the spring, notoriously the most barren
" of animal life of any of the Arctic shores,
" and the few deer that may be seen are
" generally very shy from having been
' hunted during the winter by Indians on
" the borders of the woodlands. Again,
" your correspondent says, 'the ships have
" ' been abandoned and pillaged by the
" ' Esquimaux.' In this opinion I perfectly
" agree, as far as the abandonment of the
" ships, but not that these ships were pil-
" laged by the natives. Had this been the
" case, wood would have been abundant
" among these poor people. It was not so,
" and they were reduced to the necessity of
" making their sledges of musk-ox skins,
" folded up and frozen together—an alter-
" native to which the want of wood could
" alone have reduced them. It may be as
" well here to state, for the information of
" your correspondent and others, that the
" Hudson Bay Company have, in the most
" kind manner, permitted me to devote my
" whole time, as long as requisite, to satisfy
" the questions, as far as in my power, and
" to reply to communications from the rela-

" tives and friends of the long-missing party, " instead of to complete my chart and write " up the report of my expedition for their " information. I trust that any of the rela- " tives of the lost navigators who may, in " future, wish to make severe remarks on " the mode in which I have acted, in the " very perplexing position in which I was " placed, will first do me the favour of " communicating with me, and, if I cannot " satisfy their doubts, it will then be quite " time enough to make their opinions public.

" *October* 30." " JOHN RAE.

To the Editor of the Examiner.

Sir,—The letter signed " S," and the letter of Dr. Rae, quoted by you in answer, deserve from me a few comments.

Dr. Rae deservedly takes rank with the Arctic heroes, and he is a traveller after my own fashion—simple and inexpensive, bold and enduring in his *personnel* and *matériel.* I should be sorry, therefore, to say anything to give him pain.

Had Dr. Rae " limited his belief," as you, Sir, " to the proofs of identity and death," much pain and anxiety would have been spared to us. The intrepid traveller has formed an opinion solely upon his pantomimic conversation with the Esquimaux—solely upon "the few words which pass "between two men who speak no common "language;" and is still striving to maintain that opinion, solely, and irrespective of all others, of his own knowledge of the country he is dealing with. I believe he cannot—I hope he cannot—establish that opinion.

The conclusion, as I understand it, at which Dr. Rae has arrived, is that the white men at Great Fish River had died the death of starvation and cannibalism. His premises are these. The Esquimaux had no abundance of wood, and they would have had abundance of wood if they had plundered Franklin's ships. Great Fish River is deficient of game in the spring, and it was in the spring they were said to have died.

Dr. Rae has stated in the *Times*, he has not read the "Blue Books;" and a relative of Sir John Franklin states for him, in the *Times*, that he knew not of the £.10,000 prize offered by the Government, in 1850, for the traces of The Franklin Expedition.

I can scarcely presume, therefore, to think he has ever read the humble narrative of a journey by me to the Polar Sea by Great Fish River, or a History of the Esquimaux, by me, in the Journal of the Ethnological Society of London.

Further, that he is not acquainted with my "*cache*" at Montreal Island, notwithstanding constant reference has been made to that *cache*, not only in the daily press, but within the walls of the Geographical Society; and notwithstanding Mr. Thomas Simpson visited it to correct his longitude and raise a memorial of his visit.

These are Mr. Thomas Simpson's words:—

" On the 16th we directed our course, with
" flags flying, to Montreal Island. Directed
" by M^c^Kay[34], our people soon found a
" deposit among the rocks, containing two
" bags of pemican, several pounds of choco-
" late, two canisters of gunpowder, a box
" of percussion caps, and a japanned tin
" vasculum, inclosing three large fish-hooks.
" The pemican, or *taureau*, as the voyagers
" call it, was literally alive; and it was
" wittily remarked, '*l'Isle de Montreal sera*

[34] My Steersman.

" ' *bientot, peuplée de jeunes taureaux.*' The " minor articles, Mr. Dease and I took pos- " session of as memorials of having break- " fasted on the identical spot where the " tent of our less successful precursor (Sir " George Back) stood that very day five " years before. Finding it impossible to " reconcile Sir George Back's longitude, I " have adhered to my own observations, " and thus the extent of our discoveries is " diminished by twenty-five miles[35]."

I can assure Dr. Rae that he is wrong in all his premises. First, the Esquimaux have no use for wood, for they do not use wood for fuel, the sea-oil is their fuel; for they do not use wood for boat-building, the walrus-skin is their boat; and, as the little wood they use, together with walrus ivory, in the manufacture of implements of the chase, is so contrived as to return to the owner, we may almost say they do not use wood even for the manufacture of implements of the chase. Moreover, Dr. Rae seems to forget that the Esquimaux describe the forty white men as dragging a boat, and, of

[35] Narrative of Discoveries on the North Coast of America, by Thomas Simpson, 8th Jan., 1843, p. 370.

course, its complement of oars and masts; and, as forty men could not get into one boat, at least, such a boat as Franklin would select to pass up rapids and cascades, there were most likely two boats, aye, and even three boats, enough wood for several generations of the Esquimaux of that locality. There is also the Victory steam ship, left by Sir John Ross, close by.

Then, Dr. Rae states:—"That portion of "country near to, and on which a portion "of Sir John Franklin's party was seen, is, "in the spring, notoriously the most barren "of animal life of any of the Arctic shores, "and the few deer that may be seen are "generally very shy, from having been "hunted during the winter by Indians on "the borders of the Woodlands." Dr. Rae must excuse my saying this is mere assumption, and altogether gratuitous on his part. He is not justified in saying any such thing. Dr. Rae, it has to be borne in mind, has never put his foot on a single inch of the ground under consideration. He knows only of Great Fish River by hearsay. The only three travellers who have visited the Polar coast-line between Coppermine

River and Great Fish River are, Sir George Back, Mr. Thomas Simpson, and myself. The three narratives of these travellers are published, and all shew the country to be teeming with animal life, even up to the great human family.

The Esquimaux are very numerous in the vicinity of Great Fish River, and as we know nothing of their moral and intellectual character, they may turn out in the end to be as treacherous as the Esquimaux of Mackenzie River. There is not a doubt in my mind that the small seal the 40 white men traded from the Esquimaux, was for the known beauty of its young skin, and that thirty-five of the forty white men were subsequently murdered by treachery; that of the five white men on Montreal Island, one of them was Sir John Franklin himself, and that he had separated, with his four companions, from the other thirty-five, for the purpose of depositing in the *King cache* a memorial of his visit, which had been his practice year after year, as Captain M'Clure visited the *Parry Sandstone.* The Esquimaux, taking advantage of the separation, fell upon the thirty-five white men at Point

Ogle, who were most assuredly without fire-arms, and massacred them — five only escaping—and then blockading Montreal Island, starved out Franklin and his four companions.

17, *Savile Row, Nov. 8th*, 1854. RICHARD KING.

The Sun thus replied to Dr. Rae in a leading article:—

We publish to-day a letter from Dr. Rae, in answer to the letter of the brother of one of The Franklin Expedition.

We confess that we do not like the tone of Dr. Rae's defence. We read him on October 30th thus:—

" I trust that any of the relatives of " the lost navigators, who may in future " wish to make severe remarks on the " mode in which I have acted, in the very " perplexing position in which I was " placed, will first do me the favour of " communicating with me, and if I cannot " satisfy their doubts, it will then be quite " time enough to make their opinions " public. Such would be the more fair " and satisfactory course."

And on the 26th, four days previously,

in the plan which he had submitted to the Board of Admiralty, down Great Fish River to the spot where he says the tragedy of The Franklin Expedition was enacted, we read him thus:—

"Permit me to impress upon you the "necessity of haste in setting these expe- "ditions in train."

Now, let us ask Dr. Rae whether the devoted brother of one of the crew of The Franklin Expedition is not as much entitled to "haste" as Dr. Rae is entitled to "haste?" If Dr. Rae places so high a value upon his own judgment that he has a right to stand paramount, we do not. Dr. Rae may be in "haste" to go, or get some friend to go, for it is all the same thing, by Great Fish River, to bury the remains of The Franklin Expedition. Yet he is pained beyond measure because a devoted brother is in "haste" to clear, not one of his own flesh and blood only, but 137 other noble souls, from the horrid crime of man-eating. Dr. Rae goes on to say:—"It may "be as well here to state, for the informa- "tion of your correspondent," addressing *The Times*, "and others, that the authorities

" of the Hon. Hudson Bay Company have, " in the most kind manner, permitted me " to devote my whole time, as long as " requisite, to satisfy the questions, as far " as in my power, and to reply to com- " munications from the relatives and " friends of the long-missing party, instead " of to complete my chart, and write up " the report of my expedition for their " information."

Let Dr. Rae set to work at once and complete his report, and leave it to others to answer questions as to whether he was justified in saying that—" from the muti- " lated state of many of the corpses, and " the contents of the kettles, it is *evident* " that our wretched countrymen had been " driven to the last resource—cannibalism " —as a means of prolonging existence."

Apart from the statement, which is harrowing enough, there is something about the language " wretched countrymen," to which we strongly object. We are fully aware of all and everything Dr. Rae has done—we award to him all credit for boldness of character and unwearied industry, but we have some doubt of his judgment. We wait for his report to read his proceedings by. "To have verified," he says, "the report which I brought "home would, I believe, have been no "difficult matter; but it could not be done "by my party in any other way than by "passing another winter in Repulse Bay, "and making another journey over the ice "and snow in the spring of 1855."

This may or may not be. It is precisely what we want to know. All he has placed on record in *The Times* is thus expressed:— "During my journey from Repulse Bay "this spring over the ice, with the view of "completing the survey, &c."

There is no mention of date—no light by which we can judge whether he could or could not have verified the verdict he has unhesitatingly passed upon The Franklin Expedition.

Dr. Rae's knowledge of the country over which he has travelled is evidently very limited. He must bear in mind that there are other doctors besides himself, who have gone over the country of his travels—highly educated, highly accomplished, and highly enterprising men—Dr. Sir John Richardson and Dr. King. These distinguished travellers may possibly have their eye upon Dr. Rae. Dr. Sir John Richardson will hardly let his old companion in adventure, Sir John Franklin, die a cannibal without more distinct proof. We will answer for Dr. King. As to Dr. Rae's "reason for "returning from Pelly Bay without having "effected the survey he had contemplated, "to prevent the risk of more valuable lives "being sacrificed in a useless search," we must express our doubts. Pelly Bay is a "Gordian Knot" which we mean to have a hand in unravelling at a more convenient opportunity.

My letter in the *Examiner* would not have been written if Dr. Rae's statement to the Hudson Bay Company had been in existence at the time. The man who could write on so sacred a subject as the fate of The Franklin Expedition, one statement to the Government and another to the commercial Company who employed him, the one utterly at variance with the other, was totally unworthy of the time I then wasted upon him. I had all along associated Dr. Rae with the members of the medical profession who have distinguished themselves as travellers, such as Park, Oudenay, Richardson, McCormick, Daniel, Leichardt, and Kane; but I now find, and I rejoice in the discovery, that he is what he signs himself—a "C.F.," that is to say a Chief Factor, a *trader* in the service of the Hudson Bay Company.

So far as Dr. Rae's letter to the Admiralty is concerned, there can be no question that the general construction put upon that letter was, that in his *homeward*, not *outward* journey, he had learned the particulars he has given us. He not only accepts this construction, but uses it to his advantage. In sending his statement to *The Times*, he introduces the subject to that paper by a letter in which he states—"During my "journey *from* Repulse Bay, &c.[36]" Again, "I have no doubt from the careful habits "of these people (Esquimaux) that almost "every article which these unhappy suf- "ferers had preserved could be recovered,

[36] "The Times," 23 Oct. '54.

" but *I thought it better to come home direct " with the intelligence I had obtained, than " to run the risk of having to spend another " winter in the snow*[37]."

Again, in answer to the letter of "E. J. H.[38]" in *The Times*, and that of " S.[39]" in the *Examiner*, he states: "To have verified the " reports which I brought home would, I " believe, have been no difficult matter, but " it could not possibly be done by my party " in any other way than by passing another " winter at Repulse Bay, and making " another journey over the ice and snow in " the spring of 1855. My reason for re- " turning from Repulse Bay without having " effected the survey I had contemplated " was to prevent the risk of more valuable " lives being sacrificed in a useless search " in portions of the Arctic Seas, hundreds " of miles distant from the sad scene where " so many of the long-lost party terminated."

My reason for placing Dr. Rae's letters, the one to the Admiralty, and the other to the Hudson Bay Company, side by side, is

[37] "The Times," 23 Oct. '54. [38] *Idem*, 26 Oct. '54.

[39] "Examiner,, 4 Nov. '54.

now apparent. It was in his *outward* and not *homeward* journey he learnt the melancholy particulars of the fate of The Franklin Expedition. Read him in his statement to the Hudson Bay Company:—"From the
" head of Pelly Bay—which is a bay, spite
" of Sir F. Beaufort's opinion to the con-
" trary, I crossed 60 miles of land in a
" westerly direction, traced the west shore
" from Castor and Pollux River to Cape
" Porter, and I could have got within 30
" or 40 miles of Bellott Strait, but I thought
" it useless proceeding further, as I could
" not complete the whole."

It was then, *after* he became acquainted with the *whereabouts* of the remnant of the gallant Franklin and his noble band of adventurers, *forty in number*, that he travelled from Repulse Bay to Castor and Pollux River, a distance of 60 out of 100 miles, in a direct line, for the dead bodies of his countrymen, bleaching under the canopy of heaven. While at Castor and Pollux River, he could have harnessed his dog sledge, and in *six* or at least *eight hours* have verified the statement he has given us, which has demanded an express expedition for its verification. He would thus have spared Sir James Graham one of the many blots with which he is bedaubed as a minister of England, and he would have spared himself the disgrace which his letter in *The Times*, dated Tavistock Hotel, Covent Garden, Oct. 30, '54, reflects upon him. What! "deeply "pained and not a little surprised" at some remarks in a letter *purporting* to come from a brother of one of the officers of H.M.S. 'Terror?' Sir George Simpson, when he published Dr. Rae's statement in the *Montreal Herald* of the 21st September, 1854, little knew the mischief he was bringing upon the head of his protégé. But for Sir George Simpson, Dr. Rae's answer to "E. J. H." would have passed *current* as it has passed current up to the time of the publication of this Narrative. *Counterfeits* pass *current* for a time, until a little fingering is brought to bear upon them. Let us, then, bring a little fingering to bear upon the following quotations:—

Dr. Rae's Statement in "The Times."

To have verified the reports which I brought home would have been no difficult matter, but it could not possibly be done by my party in any other way than by passing another winter at Repulse Bay, and making another journey over the ice and snow in the spring of 1855.

Dr. Rae's Statement in the "Montreal Herald."

From the head of Pelly Bay I crossed sixty miles of land in a westerly direction, traced the West shore from Castor and Pollux River to Cape Porter, and I could have got within thirty or forty miles of Bellott Strait, but I thought it useless proceeding further, as I could not complete the whole.

"Murder will out," though hidden for a time at the bottom of a well, as the Admiralty have learned to their horror, if the word "horror" is in their dictionary, in relation to The Franklin Expedition; so with Dr. Rae. Until his statement to the Hudson Bay Company turned up, he went on very well. He reined himself up and rode the high horse.

The letter of "E. J. H." "*deeply pained* "*and not a little surprised him. He could* "*have easily passed another winter at Repulse* "*Bay, and made another journey over the* "*ice and snow in the spring of* 1855, *without* "*exposure to more privations than persons* "*accustomed to the Hudson Bay Company* "*service are in the habit of enduring; but* "*he had a deeper motive in returning from* "*Repulse Bay without having effected the* "*survey he had contemplated. It was to* "*prevent the risk of valuable lives being* "*sacrificed in a useless search hundreds of* "*miles distant from where the lives of the* "*long-lost party terminated.*"

Although I had always my misgivings of Dr. Rae's ability as a traveller, I always gave him credit for enterprise and manly bearing; I am therefore astonished beyond measure that he could have written such language to "E. J. H." in the face of his statements to Sir George Simpson that he had *made the journey to* "*Castor and Pollux River, and* "*hence to Cape Porter, and he could have* "*got within* 30 *or* 40 *miles of Bellott Strait,* "*but that he thought it useless proceeding* "*further, as he could not complete the whole.*"

Then his "*reason for returning from Re-* "*pulse Bay without having effected the survey* "*he had contemplated, to prevent the risk of* "*valuable lives*" is not the fact. His object was to reach Bellott Strait, but that the approach of winter drove him back. Can anything be more clear on this point than the following extract from his letter to Sir George Simpson?:—"*Never in my former* "*Arctic journeys had I met with such an* "*accumulation of obstacles. Fogs, storms,* "*rough ice, and deep snow we had to fight* "*against*[40]."

R. K. (Richard King) has not the slightest hesitation, therefore, in telling Dr. Rae that "E. J. H." (Rev. E. J. Hodgson) is perfectly right in stating that "*he has been deeply* "*reprehensible in not verifying the report* "*which he received from the Esquimaux;*" with the addition that the tale as a whole, seeing that it was *pantomime* the Esquimaux who gave the information was playing, is indeed a wonderful tale. For instance, 40 white men travelling over the ice; 30 dead at Point Ogle; 5 dead at Montreal Island; and so on in detail of the minutest kind. I have played *pantomime* with the North American Indians over and over again when I had a *hungry belly* and *other hungry bellies* dependent upon me to satisfy, therefore

[40] "Montreal Herald," 21 Sept., 1844.—And all this after he had been within 40 miles of the Death-spot of The Franklin Expedition.

desirous of being particularly intelligent; but I found it a hard matter to turn *pantomime* to sufficient account even to satisfy these cravings.

That he should have stood on the shore of Castor and Pollux River, his right eye directed to Point Ogle and his left eye to Montreal Island, knowing that the fate of The Franklin Expedition was to be read there, and instead of directing his steps to the tragedy before him, that he should have turned his back upon these painfully interesting lands, and have proceeded upon his paltry discovery, which if he could have made it a discovery, was utterly worthless, is a problem I will not pretend to solve. I was able to solve the problem of three centuries, the North-West Passage, in 1845, although it was not proved until 1854. I was able to point out the Death-spot of The Franklin Expedition in 1845, although it was not discovered until 1854; but Dr. Rae is a problem I cannot solve. He is a *conundrum* I *give up*. I only hope he made the journey to Castor and Pollux River, and hence to Cape Porter[41].

[41] Refer back to page 36 for an account of a previous journey.

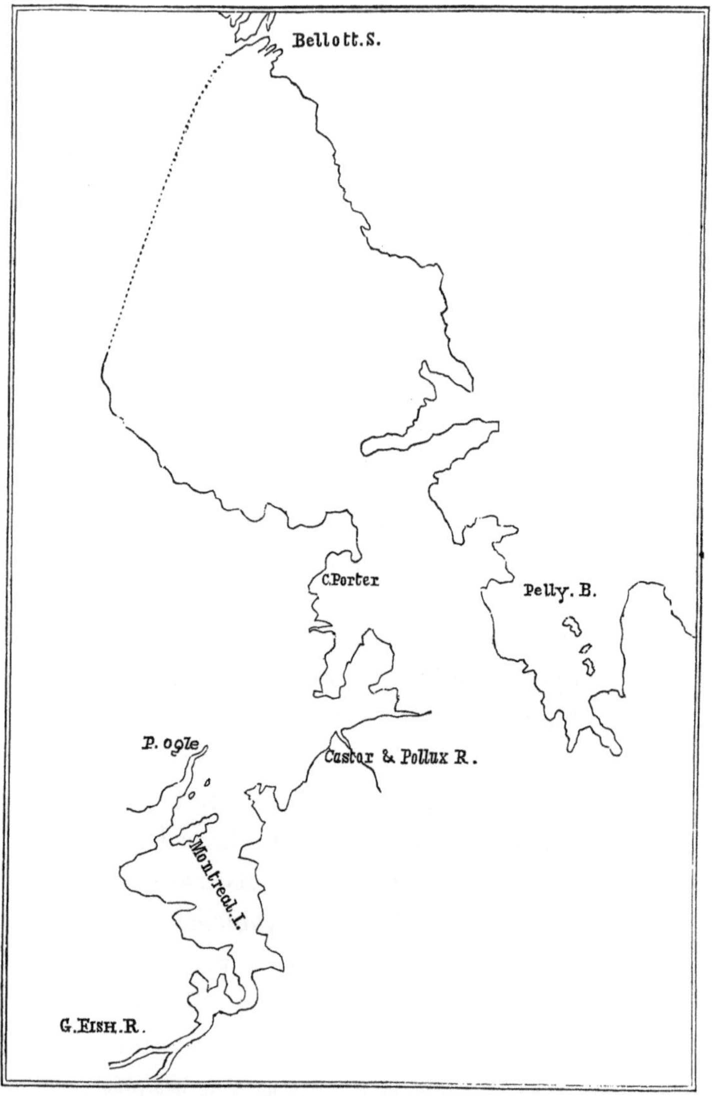
Bellott.S.
C.Porter
Pelly. B.
P. ogle
Castor & Pollux R.
Montreal.I.
G.Fish.R.

The means by which Dr. Rae became possessed of the relics of The Franklin Expedition will ever be matter of doubt in my mind; but I have no doubt a great calamity, little, if at all, short of death overtook a remnant of the gallant party at the mouth of Great Fish River.

And there can be no doubt, had the Board of Admiralty conscientiously discharged the duty imposed upon them by the Nation, that the gallant band, who reached Great Fish River, would have been restored to their families and friends, and the historian spared the necessity of recording the awful tragedy, of which the Board of Admiralty most assuredly are the cruel authors.

I have arranged the several Boards of Admiralty, who have dealt with the fate of The Franklin Expedition, in a statistical form, in order to mark the exact amount of guilt which lies at each man's door;—a very large share falls to Sir M. F. F. Berkeley, W. A. B. Hamilton, Alexander Milne, and W. F. Cowper.

Lords of the Admiralty.

1847—1854.

	Years in Office.	Years in Office.	
Alexander Milne	8	7	Sir M. F. F. Berkeley, M.P.
a. W. F. Cowper	7	5 f.	Lord John Hay.
b. J. W. Deans Dundas	5	3	Sir F. T. Baring.
c. Hyde Parker	3	3	Houston Stewart.
Sir James Graham	2	2 c.	Earl Auckland.
d. R. Saunders Dundas	2	2 e.	Henry Prescott.
Peter Richards	2	1	Duke of Northumberland.
A. Duncombe	1	1	Sir Thomas Herbert.

Phipps Hornby.
1.

Secretaries of the Admiralty.

W. A. B. Hamilton	8	5	H. G. Ward.
Ralph Osborne	2	1	Augustus Stafford.

a. President of the Board of Health.
b. Command in the Black Sea.
c. Dead.
d. Command in the Baltic Sea.
e. Superintendent Portsmouth Dockyard.
f. Superintendent Plymouth Dockyard.

The present Board of Admiralty is composed of:—

Sir C. Wood, Bart., M.P.	Peter Richards.
Sir M. F. F. Berkeley, M.P.	Alexander Milne.
Henry Eden.	Sir Robert Peel, Bart., M.P.

Young Admiralty, that is to. say, Sir Robert Peel and Henry Eden, had better look well to Sir M. F. F. Berkeley and

Alexander Milne, if they desire to be of service to their country.

Captain Grover brought the deaths of Colonel Stoddart and Captain Conolly home to Lord Aberdeen, and entitled his narrative "The Bokhara Victims," and, as I have brought the death of The Franklin Expedition home to the Board of Admiralty, I might very properly, entitle mine "The Polar Victims."

We are indebted to the London Press for the *light* which brought the horrors of the Crimea face to face with those who enacted them,—which led the House of Commons to hurl them from the posts which they held with so much discredit to themselves and to the Nation. We are also indebted to the London Press for their powerful advocacy of the search by Great Fish River, and for their no less powerful condemnation of the neglect of that search. I have recorded the terms of the advocacy, here follow the terms of the condemnation :—

The *Examiner*, 28th October, '54.

There is no longer any doubt of the melancholy death of Sir John Franklin and his companions. To the roll-call of perished heroes, to the lists now daily swelling with noble names, of brave men battling against fearful odds, and dying in the performance of their duty, are to be added the names of the Arctic voyagers. The sad assurance might have reached us at a moment less distracted by other anxieties and sorrows, but it comes not unfitly while the public sympathy is keenly awakened to the claims of all who imperil life for high and unselfish aims. Almost simultaneously with the fate of so many who left us six months since to perish in the tents at Varna, on the heights of the Alma, or before the walls of Sebastopol, we learn the fate of the devoted band who departed ten years ago to face a far more terrible foe, and, after more than three years of unspeakable suffering, have left behind them but the memory of that unflinching enterprise and endurance, that resolute perseverance, that moral and physical courage, that hardihood unappalled and discipline undisturbed by the most frightful dangers which we take to be peculiar to English seamen.

Of the correctness of the testimony, oral

and circumstantial, which Dr. Rae has brought home, we limit our belief to the proofs of identity and death. The evidence is quite imperfect as to the manner of the death, or as to the shocking incidents assumed to have preceded it; but for the rest, the pieces of silver plate, the crests and initials, the watches, telescopes, and guns, tell sufficiently the terrible story. It is also borne out by the Esquimaux accounts, which neither is there any reason to doubt, of the exhausted state of the little band. At once marvellous and mortifying is it, that, in a vicinity so attainable, so known, so likely to be visited as the position of the magnetic pole, the lost wanderers could neither have been met with, or directed towards reaching supplies. But unfortunately every effort at discovery or help, up to the period when all such ceased to be useful, was directed to the sea and its shores, although the abandonment of the ships and betaking of the crews to land passage was a circumstance so naturally to be looked for. The Admiralty people were too romantic in their conjectures. Ships and men, it was thought, must have disappeared up one of those mysterious and perilous avenues that strike northwards towards the pole; and that the starving band should have been prosaically sought for on the bank of Great Fish River was in the contemplation of none.

Of none in authority. But let us do justice to Dr. King, who, with a humane perseverance worthy of better success, has vainly urged upon successive Governments, ever since 1847, that the expeditions in search of our lost countrymen should take that exact course which we now see too late would have led upon their track. In 1847 he wrote to Lord Grey to point out Great Fish River as the high and ice-free road to the land where the missing expedition was likely to be found. In the same year he implored to have his services joined to those of Sir James Ross and Sir John Richardson, using these remarkable words:—

"It is a service in which I can act independently of Sir James Clarke Ross, and independently of Sir John Richardson; and Sir James Clarke Ross and Sir John Richardson, it is already arranged, are to act independently of each other. Sir James Clarke Ross's knowledge of Barrow Strait—Sir John Richardson's knowledge of the Mackenzie and the Coppermine Rivers—and my knowledge of Great Fish River and its estuary, will be so many guarantees that the work to be done will be done well; and this state of independence will insure a large amount of effort, even though it were merely in a spirit of emulation."

Two years later (some six or eight months before the date of the now ascertained calamity) he renewed his applications. He wrote letters to Lady Franklin to tell her she was ill advised, and, with all the vehemence of personal entreaty, besieged successive Secretaries to the Admiralty; but Mr. Ward, Mr. Hamilton, and all the rest, returned him answers as cold and unsympathising as their chiefs, and the opportunity was lost which never was to return. Hear the Cassandra of this ill-fated business! We quote one of his last appeals:—

"All that has been done by way of search since February 1848, tends to draw closer and closer to the west land of North Somerset as the position of Sir John Franklin, and to Great Fish River as the high road to reach it. Such a plan as I proposed to their Lordships in 1848 is consequently of the utmost importance.

It would be the happiest moment of my life if their Lordships would allow me to go by my old route, Great Fish River, to attempt to save human life a second time on the shores of the Polar Sea."

It is deplorable to think that in every instance the Admiralty attempts to find our countrymen have been by far the least successful. Kennedy and poor Bellott were near upon the track, but theirs was a private expedition, and not undertaken till a year too late. When we discussed the subject in this journal at the close of 1849, we urged the necessity of then making a final effort, and, considering that the chances would not warrant the risk of another expedition, we held that it should have been planned on such a scale as completely to scour the track, both by land and sea, in which the clearest judgments might see the probabilities of success. More than two years had then passed beyond the time to which the ships were victualled, and we believed it to be our last gleam of rational hope. It is now proved to have been so.

On the details of what our lamented countrymen have suffered we forbear to dwell. It was into no unknown perils Sir

John Franklin ventured. Nearly thirty years earlier, and again after an interval of six or seven years, his indomitable spirit had been tried in the same disastrous scenes. The language contains no records of enterprise and endurance surpassing those of his two journeys to the shores of the Polar Sea, and to them we have but to turn to obtain no dim or imperfect image of the terror of his final journey, or of what we may hope to have been the merciful assuagements vouchsafed to it. "At this period we avoided " as much as possible conversing upon " the hopelessness of our situation, and " generally endeavoured to lead the con- " versation towards our future prospects " in life. With the decay of our strength, " in fact, our minds decayed, and we were " no longer able to bear the contemplation " of the horrors that surrounded us. Each " of us excused himself from so doing by a " desire of not shocking the feelings of the " others. We were sensible of one another's " weakness of intellect, though blind to our " own. Yet we were calm and resigned " to our fate, not a murmur escaped us, " and we were punctual and fervent in our

" addresses to the Supreme Being." When these affecting words were written, the writer and his companions were so nearly face to face with death, that the delay of but another day in their relief might then have anticipated the national sorrow which now makes sacred the memory of Sir John Franklin.

Spectator, 28th October, '54.

The fate of the Franklin Expedition has this week received a new and gloomy light. Thirty-five dead bodies have been discovered by Esquimaux at the mouth of Great Fish River. As early as 1847 Dr. King pointed out this very spot as the path by which to seek them. The spring of 1849 was the natural termination of Franklin's supplies on the longest safe calculation; and in a note by the Lords of the Admiralty published in 1847, they declared that if no accounts were received of Franklin by the end of that year, active steps must be taken in the search. No serious apprehensions, however, were then felt. Sir George Back declared in January 1848 that " he could " not bring himself to entertain more than

" ordinary anxiety for the safety and return " of Sir John Franklin." Suggestions were made for sending the search directly after Franklin by Davis Strait, or by Great Fish River, or by Mackenzie River; but we remember how these steps were delayed or partially carried out, and how a controversy was carried on at a subsequent date, as to whether the expedition must not have perished entirely. We now learn that a considerable number of the party at least survived until the spring, probably until May 1850. We have yet no certain proof that the whole party had expired.

It is evident that if the quest had been prosecuted by those who had been sent out to assist them early and widely enough their path had been crossed. Dr. King pointed out, in 1847, the exact path taken by Franklin as the one in which he might be met or crossed.

Franklin had made some way towards that same part of the globe in which he had previously braved death. There was a period in 1821 when some of his companions actually succumbed to that death by starvation and hardships which the others escaped when they believed themselves beyond hope; and now a band of Englishmen, headed by the same officer, returned almost to the same spot. They were near the mouth of that river near whose source was their rendezvous of Fort Enterprise in 1821. How many changes had taken place in the interval! Franklin was a generation older; he had grown deaf; but he had not lost any resolution. He had different companions, but they appear to have been not less faithful. He had come by the sea and not by land, yet he was doomed to the same hardships. Nothing is more affecting, or at the same time more elevating, than the narrative of men travelling sometimes knee-deep in snow for miles on miles, for days and months, feeding on the most precarious, the basest kind of food; sometimes depending upon the gun, picking from the rocks the noxious weed *tripe de roche*, gathering carrion of the past season, or going back to the old haunts to feast on the marrow of bones thrown away in the year before, on pieces of hide and their own shoes; deliberately measuring out these horrible supplies, calculating their strength for days upon such sustenance; and all the while sustaining each other throughout with comfort, with religious thoughts, with example. They found themselves—and the confession comes with an unspeakable dignity of candour—growing at times under the pressure of infirmity hasty and irritable. The man who felt firm in his own courage was daunted at the gaunt face and deep sepulchral voice of his companions. We have yet no certain proof that the whole party had expired. The original number was one hundred and thirty-eight; three were buried at Beechy Island; forty were seen alive by the Esquimaux, thirty-five bodies are found at Great Fish River—a statement which still leaves five of the forty unaccounted for; and some eighty or ninety more of the entire party are unmentioned.

Atlas, 28th October, '54.

If the public had not made up its mind that Sir John Franklin and his companions have been beyond human help, the account recently communicated of the alleged fate of part of his expedition would have been received with greater doubt and reservation than has yet been evinced. It is stated that the Government mean to send out another expedition to make further inquiries; but why did they not long ago search the spot where the bodies are alleged to have been discovered? They were repeatedly urged to do so by Dr. King, the well known Arctic voyager, who gave good reasons for believing that Sir John Franklin might be found in this very place, and offered to take charge of an inexpensive expedition to proceed overland to North Somerset and Great Fish River, with which localities he was well acquainted. The offers to the Colonial Office to seek for the missing party were constantly repeated, and at the close of the year met with a formal official refusal, against which decision Dr. King earnestly remonstrated, and again in February 1850 renewed his proposition, this time directing it to the Admiralty. The reply to this was that the "Admiralty had no intention of "altering their arrangements," and thus Sir John Franklin and his party were practically left to their fate; and when the country holds an inquest upon their remains, it can only find the verdict that they died of official pigheadedness and Admiralty neglect.

Daily News, 26th October, '54.

The proposal of Dr. King to explore the shores and seas to the south of the line of research pursued by the naval expeditions was systematically pooh-poohed. The circumstance that Franklin and his crews having lost their ships, might be struggling over the ice to the South, was wilfully and systematically ignored; yet the statements which have been collected from the Esquimaux, and the articles picked up among them, make it certain that an overland boat-expedition descending Great Fish River, had it been sent out in time, would in all probability have saved at least a remnant of the crews. To what has the error been owing? In the first place, to the tardiness of the permanent Admiralty officials in instituting the search. In the second place, to their obstinate and exclusive preference of large and costly naval expeditions, which placed the distribution of patronage in their hands, and their discouragement of less pretentious expeditions, which would not thus have gratified their jobbing propensities or vanity. In the third place, to that pedantry which would not even listen with courtesy to any but professional advice; meaning by professional, not even nautical opinion in the widest acceptation of the term, but the opinion of mere fighting nauticals. What is now known shews that in the controversies of the last seven years the landsmen have been nearer the mark than the soldiers—the sailors of the merchant service than the officers of the Royal Navy. But the favouritism of the Admiralty—its permanent officials—entrusted the research almost exclusively to the officers of the Royal Navy, listened only to their proposals, reserved for them all honours and emoluments. Thus have the *permanent* officials of the Admiralty prevented Franklin from being saved. His blood and the blood of his brave companions is on their heads!"

Observer, 29th October, '54.

"All the hopes and fears that for the

last seven years have existed on account of Sir John Franklin and his crews are now almost, if not altogether, set at rest. It appears that the very spot insisted upon by Dr. King, is the same spot where the bodies have been found. He considered, that Sir John Franklin failing in his efforts, and not being able to extricate his ships, would implicitly follow the instructions of the Admiralty, and proceed South; whilst the majority of the expeditions which have been sent out in search of the missing party, have had their routes directed, on the assumption that Sir John Franklin had disregarded his instructions. It would therefore appear, that had Dr. King's proposal been adopted in 1847, in all human probability, Sir John Franklin might have been saved. Dr. King has shewn that he knows more about Polar Discovery than any one else, for as early as 1847, in a letter to Earl Grey, he says:—'To a land journey alone can we look for success; for the failure of a land journey would be the exception of the rule, while the failure of a sea expedition would be the rule itself. To the Western Land of North Somerset, *where*

I maintain Sir John Franklin will be found, Great Fish River is the direct and only route; and although the approach to it is through a country too poor and difficult of access, to admit of the transport of provisions, it may be made the medium of communication between the lost Expedition and the civilized world.' "

The *Sun*, 23rd October, '54.

" Poor Sir John Franklin! the melancholy fate of the intrepid navigator and his gallant companions have at length been manifested. It has been more horrible than had ever been anticipated. The most glaring apprehensions have been verified; and what renders the fearful result even more deplorable is, that we now know that a large proportion of the party might have been rescued had the authorities at home displayed any degree of energy or activity. Our unfortunate countrymen struggled hard for their lives,—during five dreary winters they sustained all the accumulated horrors of the ice-bound prison. On each succeeding spring the throb of hopeful anticipation must have thrilled through their hearts, in the expectation of the succour and comfort they were never destined to receive. What stores of important and interesting information might we not have received, if even a few of these adventurous men had been restored to their expectant friends. But alas! a more awful heart-rending catastrophe than any that ever occurred under similar circumstances was about to happen. One by one they perished by the most fearful of all deaths. The strength which they had endeavoured to sustain, gradually wasted away, and the last survivor drooped and died, probably in the summer of 1850.

"The evidence by which this heart-rending narrative has been established is so clear and distinct as to leave no possible doubt as to its accuracy. The information casually obtained and the articles purchased from the Esquimax, have placed the *vexata questio* respecting the fate of Sir John Franklin and his followers beyond the possibility of doubt. These heart-rending relics will be endowed with a melancholy interest."

The *Sun*, 25th October, '54.

"We revert to the awful tragedy of the Franklin Expedition, consisting of 138 souls; a small portion only of the dreadful scene is before us; a mere moiety of the gallant band of adventurers is accounted for. Point Ogle is the resting-place of some, and Montreal Island of others. We refrain from harrowing the feelings of our readers by repeating the condition in which their honoured remains were found; we would spare them and their friends such a recital. There is, however, a blood-stain somewhere. Has every effort been made for the rescue of this noble band, we ask?—for let it be distinctly understood that there were many noble souls involved in the fate of Franklin—Crozier, Fitzjames, Stanley, Goodsir, are the names of officers well known for their talents and acquirements. Many a tear for years to come will be shed over the memory of those brave men.

"Even our own pen, stern as 'time' has made us—for we were acquainted with some of the gallant crew—loses somewhat of its steadiness as we write. Peace, everlasting peace, to them! Has every effort, we repeat, been made for the rescue of this noble band? Too happy should we be to answer *yes;* but *no.* The authorities at home—and by the authorities we mean not only the Board of Admiralty, but the Colonial Board—have sacrificed The Franklin Expedition to a perverse attachment to their own special views, imbibed from one of the most prejudiced of men, the late Sir John Barrow. We have several times warned the authorities against large sea expeditions, and urged small land journeys in the prosecution of Polar research. Dr. King, the accomplished Polar traveller, who went down Great Fish River in search of Sir John Ross, in 1833-4-5, published, at the time the search for Franklin was under consideration, a pamphlet, entitled 'Polar Sea Expeditions, and Polar Land Journeys.' Every newspaper in England supported us in urging Dr. King's Polar Land Journey down Great Fish River, in lieu of Franklin's Polar Sea Expedition. And when he found the Board of Admiralty were determined to send out Franklin by sea, he submitted to Lord Stanley (now

Lord Derby), the then Colonial Secretary, a plan for descending Great Fish River overland, so as to act in concert with Franklin by sea.

" And when the fate of Franklin became serious, Dr. King implored ! first the Colonial Board, and then the Board of Admiralty, in the most forcible language that man could pen, to allow him to go by Great Fish River to the rescue of the Franklin party. He maintained from the moment Franklin started that he would be wrecked, where in all probability he has been wrecked, on the Western land of North Somerset, and that he would make for Great Fish River, in expectation of help from home ! Poor creatures ! help from home ! Only one Polar Friend held out a helping hand. Earl Grey's answer to Dr. King's powerful appeal, as well as the appeal itself, is on record. Admiration for the one and Condemnation for the other document, was the bye-word at the time of every well-thinking man ; but now a blot is stamped upon the answer of Earl Grey which he will never be able to efface.

" The Board of Admiralty sheltered themselves under the cloak of a council, called the 'Arctic Council,' who were made, not only once, but twice, to report the utter impossibility of Franklin being anywhere in the neighbourhood of Great Fish River. The refusal of Dr. King's first offer bears date 3rd of March, 1848, and the second offer 28th February, 1850. What part did Franklin's old companion, Sir George Back, take in this decision of the Arctic Council, for he was one of its members? We are acquainted with a print entitled the 'Arctic Council,' portraits of the members of the council called together under that name—let each man now tell his own tale. We cannot put a permanent value on that council until we know this. What monster evil haunts the imagination of Sir George Back, that he should ever and anon lead us from that magnificent river, teeming with every kind of animal life, even up to the great human family?

"We think we see the poor fellows at Point Ogle and Montreal Island, daily looking up Great Fish River in expectation of assistance. The spring of 1850 was not the first spring journey they had made to Great Fish River. The spring of 1848, surely the spring of 1849 also, found them on the banks of that stream. They were evidently on the look out for assistance. Franklin certainly followed out his instructions to the letter, and as certainly looked for help in the direction it should have been made. How strange, then—how utterly unaccountable—how perfectly inexplicable it is that the 'Effort in Search' should have been everywhere but in the right direction. In fact, the 'effort' has been made upon the assumption he had gone *contrary*, and not *according*, to orders. We conclude, not only with the words of a contemporary—'Thus have the *permanent* officials of the Admiralty prevented Franklin from being saved—his blood, and the blood of his brave companions is on their heads,'—but with the addition that just so much must be borne by Earl Grey as Colonial Secretary."

The *Sun*, 31st October, '54.

"The more we reflect upon the 'fate of The Franklin Expedition,' the less we are inclined to believe that this noble band of adventurers resorted to cannibalism. No—

they never resorted to such horrors. We must have stronger proof, clearer evidence of such a state of things, before we can bring our minds to this belief.

"That The Franklin Expedition is dead, almost to a man, we have little doubt. Survivors, however, there may be still; and, some day or other, some relics, such as have been found upon the Esquimaux, may bear upon them some mark, some token of a prolonged existence.

"To our minds the 'relics' bear evidence, the most indisputable, that 'The Franklin Expedition'—at least the remnant at the mouth of Great Fish River—has died a death of violence; and it is deeply to be regretted that Dr. Rae, upon such slender evidence, should have so summarily decided their fate, and turned from Castor and Pollux River, when the distance between him and all that was mortal of our gallant immortal countrymen was *scarcely forty miles.*

"Cannibalism!—the gallant Sir John Franklin a cannibal—such men as Crozier, Fitzjames, Stanley, Goodsir, cannibals! man eating man—civilised man daring to meet his Maker in a country in which cannibalism has no place—in a condition in which the 'savages,' so called, of the Great American Continent, thank God, never dare to meet their Maker—in a part of the world where the severest punishment is sure to be his doom, *an ignominious death* and *no grave.* Such is the law of the Red man.

"In this state of feeling we turned to the narratives of the Expedition in search of Sir John Ross down Great Fish River. We began with Dr. King's narrative, which we pronounced at the time of its publication to be 'full of bold adventure and stirring incident.' We quote to-day what he has said of his dealings, or rather the dealings of his chief, Sir George Back, with the Esquimaux—with those interesting, but, as it has often been found, treacherous members of the great human family. And we say, with the devoted brother of one of the crew of the Terror, in his letter, published in our impression of yesterday, from *The Times* of the same day, that 'Dr. Rae has been deeply reprehensible, either in not verifying the reports which he received from the Esquimaux, or if that was absolutely out of the question, in publishing the details of that report, resting as they do on grounds most weak and unsatisfactory. He had far better have kept silent altogether than have given us a story which, while it pains the feelings of many, must be very insufficient for all.' "

July 28th, 1834,—" Descried a party of Esquimaux, tented on the eastern boundary of a fall, who, as soon as they perceived us, commenced running to and fro in the greatest confusion. Perceiving it was our intention to land, they approached the boat, nine in number, and having formed themselves into a semicircle, commenced an address in a loud tone of voice, elevating and depressing both their arms at the same time, a sign of peace. They motioned us to put off from the shore, and at the same time uttered some unintelligible words, with a wildness of gesticulation that clearly shewed they were under the highest state of excitement. At the sound of *tima*, peace; *kabloons*, white people—they ceased yelling, and one and all laid down their spears, and commenced alternately patting their breasts and pointing to heaven. After this manifestation of their peaceful intentions, we landed and shook them heartily by the hand[42]."

A graphic account of this race follows, but our present purpose compels us to pass on to more important notices of this "race of fishermen."

[42] Narrative of a journey down Great Fish River, in search of Sir John Ross, in 1833-4-5. By Dr. King. Vol. ii., p. 68.

August 22nd, 1834.—"Reached the 'Fall' where the Esquimaux were first discovered. To our great astonishment, they had disappeared. This was the more singular, as we parted with them on the most friendly terms[43]."

August 26th, 1834.—"Reached our *cache* of two bags of pemican. It had evidently been opened, and the contents examined, though carefully covered up again, which was attributed to the Esquimaux[44]."

August 22.—"Opening the view of Lake Franklin, the Esquimaux were perceived flying in the utmost consternation to the far-distant hills, where they could be just made out with our telescopes as living objects. Their tents were deserted and their canoes secreted; conduct so different from that of our first interview that we were convinced something extraordinary must have taken place. Nor could this be in any way accounted for until our arrival in England, when it was ascertained the three men despatched to Mount Barrow, whose evasive manner at the time gave indications that something unusual had occurred, fell in, during their march, with a party of Esquimaux and for an instant retreated. The natives, in following them, fired a few arrows, upon which the men turned and discharged their guns, killed three of the party, and probably wounded others, it being the practice with the voyagers to load their fowling-pieces with two balls, so as to give them a double chance of securing their game. The natives thoroughly dismayed at seeing their countrymen fall around them, fled in the greatest disorder, and the men, equally alarmed, betook themselves to flight also.

[43] Idem, pp. 4-6. [44] Idem, p. 67.

"It is a lamentable fact that this ill-fated people have hitherto met with nothing but merciless warfare from those *whites* who have visited their lands. It is to be hoped this sad example will operate as a warning to future travellers never to send a party of men for any distance in a newly-discovered country, without one or other of the officers composing the party accompanying them. A practice exists with the Esquimaux to fire blunt arrows in token of their peaceful intentions; which, in all probability, was the case in this instance, and their friendly conduct at our first interview justifies the correctness of the assumption. "A depression of spirits (remarks Sir George Back,) in the men who visited Mount Barrow was observed for some days previously to our leaving the coast; and it increased as they approached the site of the Esquimaux encampment to so great an extent that a gloom spread itself, as if by infection, over the rest of the party, nor could it be dispelled without a glass of rum[45]."

"The Esquimaux, had they been inclined, might have murdered us in our beds with the greatest ease for we were so little apprehensive of danger, that the night-watch had for some time been discontinued. That some of the party were in a far less happy state of mind was evinced by the gloom Sir George Back perceived amongst them. Ignorant of this circumstance, and considering no good could arise from any further interview, we neither crossed over to that side of the river where the natives were encamped, nor made the least signs to attract their notice, which must have very much increased their

[45] Back's Journey to the Polar Sea.

suspicions of our amicable intentions. On leaving the rapids a number of iron hoops were placed on a pile of stones, together with ribands of various colours, awls, fish-hooks, brass rings, and beads, which, of course, would be construed into treachery on our part, for the purpose of alluring them across the river that they might fall an easier prey. During the whole of the 23rd August the Esquimaux were distinctly seen, by the aid of our telescopes, watching our motions and hiding their *kieyacks* (canoes) the sign of war."

"August 29th.—"At Lake Macdougall several fresh marks, tipped with newly-gathered moss, were perceptible on shore; we landed and found several tracks of men and dogs imprinted on the sand. We had scarcely embarked, when the Esquimaux slowly raised themselves from behind the rocks. A little further on we came in sight of ten tents, surrounded by men, women, and children, altogether amounting to about seventy or eighty souls. The women and children instantly fled to the rocks for protection, but the men awaited us along the shore, uttering some unintelligible words, and making the same friendly motions as the former party. Sir George Back declined the interview as was his practice —tactics, now that we are aware of the unfortunate attack upon the first party, the very worst that could have been adopted. This was the last time these people were seen, and it is much to be feared we left them with a very unfavourable impression[46]."

To the Editor of the *Sun*, 28th October, 1854.

"Sir,—Can any practical mind read the

[46] Narrative of a journey down Great Fish River, in search of Sir John Ross, in 1833-4-5. By Dr. King. Vol. ii., pp. 66-67.

clear views taken by Dr. King, and on calm reflection deny the guilt that lies at the Admiralty door, under the reign of the Admiral of the Black Sea[47] ?—for it was under his *regime* that the cold, apathetic neglect took place; and many that heard Dr. King's lectures will remember the many predictions that since 1849 have come true respecting the fate of Franklin; and that by the jobbing selfishness, the fighting for honours—poor Franklin would be left in the long run to his fate to die of starvation. In the 'annals of the Admiralty culpability' this is the blackest picture. Dr. King pointed out the ease with which communication could be made by Great Fish River, to those going out in search by sea;—and all these were so simple in the using, so inexpensive, that no barrier could have been made, but the dire jealousy of a self-conceited body of men, who must have their own ways and ignorant theories against the energetic and practical views of men of expanded mind, such as Dr. King. His writings now will be valued by every good, unprejudiced mind who reads; but, alas!

[47] Admiral Deans Dundas.

like the 'rotten food' under the same rule, it will be quashed, and 'dead men tell no tales,' or woe betide those who were in power when The Franklin Expedition left on their ill-fated trip. 'The tin cases of carrion,' like the knife of the slayer, lying in hundreds, and the thousands sunk since in the ocean, to thinking minds is quite enough. But, sir, allow me to point out that those men appear to be but a portion of Franklin's crews; for there cannot be a doubt in my mind but they had divided the body, some going one way and some another, so that, if one party was successful, it would send relief to the others; and that should stimulate us. Whatever he may do now, cost what it may, though millions, it will never, never wash off the cruel stain that now blackens the Admiralty of Lord John Russell. I do not wish to speak harshly of men in office; but I cannot hide the truth now, or be afraid to speak out against those who have so recklessly disregarded a solemn duty to the public, as they have done, and allowed parties to interfere for private jobbing, which I know was done (and the Blue Books can shew several matters in corroboration of Dr. King's assertions, as well as other cases of gross and culpable negligence in not sending out proper men earlier than was done), and the rejection of means and plans offered to the Admiralty; but with cold, insulting, official buffoonery, these practical philanthropic men were coolly insulted and derided. How long conduct such as this the British nation will submit to remains to be seen. Our country is falling to pieces by party jobbing —filling places and appointing officers from 'incapables' and 'old worn-out men,' kept on the staff when they ought to have retired even on a pension—for, truly, the pension is but the first and last expense.

"Yours truly,

"ONE BEHIND THE CURTAIN."

Cassell's Illustrated Family Paper, 2nd Dec. '54.

"Had Dr. King's services been accepted by the Board of Admiralty, he would have gone straight to where the remains of The Franklin Expedition have since been found —that he did not, lies at the door of Sir George Back."

The *Medical Times*, 4th November, '54.

The report of Dr. Rae upon the traces of Franklin's Expedition furnishes another instance of the sad results of the neglect of the advice of members of our profession by men in power. Ever since 1847, Dr. King has urged upon successive Governments, with a pertinacity only to be excused by the humane desire to save the devoted band of Arctic heroes, that the Expeditions sent by the Admiralty were sent in a wrong direction, and that they should take the very course which would have led them upon the exact spot where Dr. Rae's intelligence would lead us to believe the bones of our missing countrymen remain. In 1847 he wrote to Lord Grey that Great Fish River might be the road to the spot where Franklin was to be found. Two years after, several months before the spring of 1850—the spring when the Esquimaux are said to have seen the forty English—he besieged the Admiralty with applications which proved fruitless. Here is a sentence from one of his appeals:—" It " would be the happiest moment of my life "if their Lordships would allow me to go "by my old route Great Fish River to attempt to save human life a second time "on the shores of the Polar Sea."

Though rather out of the scope of a Medical Journal, the Editor of the *Medical Times* devoted a leading article in 1849 to an advocacy of Dr. King's plan of going down Great Fish River in search of Franklin. The time will come when such facts as these will convince even the most obstinate of Government officials that the advice of medical men cannot be disregarded without public loss. There is a great deal of truth in the following remarks in the *Examiner* :—

"The French say," observes the able writer, "that the medical profession has achieved for itself no adequate honour or reputation in England. In France, during the last half-century, there is no Council Board, no Administration, no Society, in which the medical profession has not found itself represented; whether at the Court of the Sovereign, or among the Peerage, or in the Legislature. Physicians of the Institute take their place naturally among the first of the land. Their views, their discoveries, their cures, their professional ideas and suggestions, must be listened to, cannot be neglected, and may never be treated as intrusive: nor had Napoleon fewer physicians and surgeons for friends, councillors, and dignitaries of State, than he had of any other profession. But in England, all such interests find themselves either unrepresented, or not represented worthily, and the best of her physicians is good only to amass money, or at the highest get a baronetcy. What important or salutary medical influence has made itself felt in the public administration since the wounds of Waterloo were healed? and where, in all those years, except to born lords or baronets, have we had the means of looking for sanitary wisdom or suggestion? For answer, we are referred to the whole history of our sanitary and medical administration. Provided only a man be born baronet or lord, we are ready to accept him for a born scavenger and born physician as well; nor can any amount of science or learning be esteemed paramount in our regard, except the science of addressing and managing constituencies, or the knack of palavering either House."

The absolute necessity of sending an expedition to the mouth of Great Fish River was now evident, and, as it appeared to me to be not possible that the Board of Admiralty could by any pretext whatever pass me over as the person best fitted to search Point Ogle and Montreal Island for the remains of The Franklin Party, seeing that I had always marked out that spot as the last resting place of the party, I forwarded to the First Lord of the Admiralty, Sir James Graham, with as little delay as possible, a copy of the whole of my correspondence with the Government on the fate of the gallant adventurers, together with the following note.

To the Secretary to the Admiralty.

Sir,—I beg to enclose a copy of my correspondence with the Government "on the Fate of The Franklin Expedition[48]."

It is my intention immediately to offer my services to the Colonial Board, to descend Great Fish River in search of the remains of The Franklin Expedition; and, if that Board declines the offer, then to the Admiralty Board.

I have the honour to be,

Your faithful servant,

17, *Savile Row*, 26 *October*, '54. RICHARD KING.

And in order still further to impress my Lords Commissioners of the Admiralty with the position in which I stood in relation to the Great Polar Question, I also transmitted

[48] See back for Correspondence, p. 5 to 82.

to them a copy of my correspondence with them when The Franklin Expedition was fitting out for its ill-fated trip,—written with the view of persuading them to allow me to act *by land* in concert with Sir John Franklin *by sea.*

To the Secretary to the Admiralty.

Sir,—I transmit for the information of my Lords Commissioners of the Admiralty a copy of my correspondence with their Lordships bearing date respectively 21 Dec. '44;—8 Jan. '45;—31 Jan. '45. There was no Sir Robert Harry Inglis in those days so this correspondence has no place in the Blue Books.

The *Lithographed Conjectural Chart*, illustrative of the correspondence, bears, in indelible characters, not only the position of the "Great Polar Passage," discovered by Sir R. M'Clure; but the Atlantic outlet of that "Great Polar Passage" through Jones Sound discovered by Sir E. Belcher.

The *Actual Chart* of 27 Oct. '54, now about to issue from the Hydrographer to the Admiralty, is doubtless *more ornamental*,

DR KINGS CONJECTURAL CHART 1845

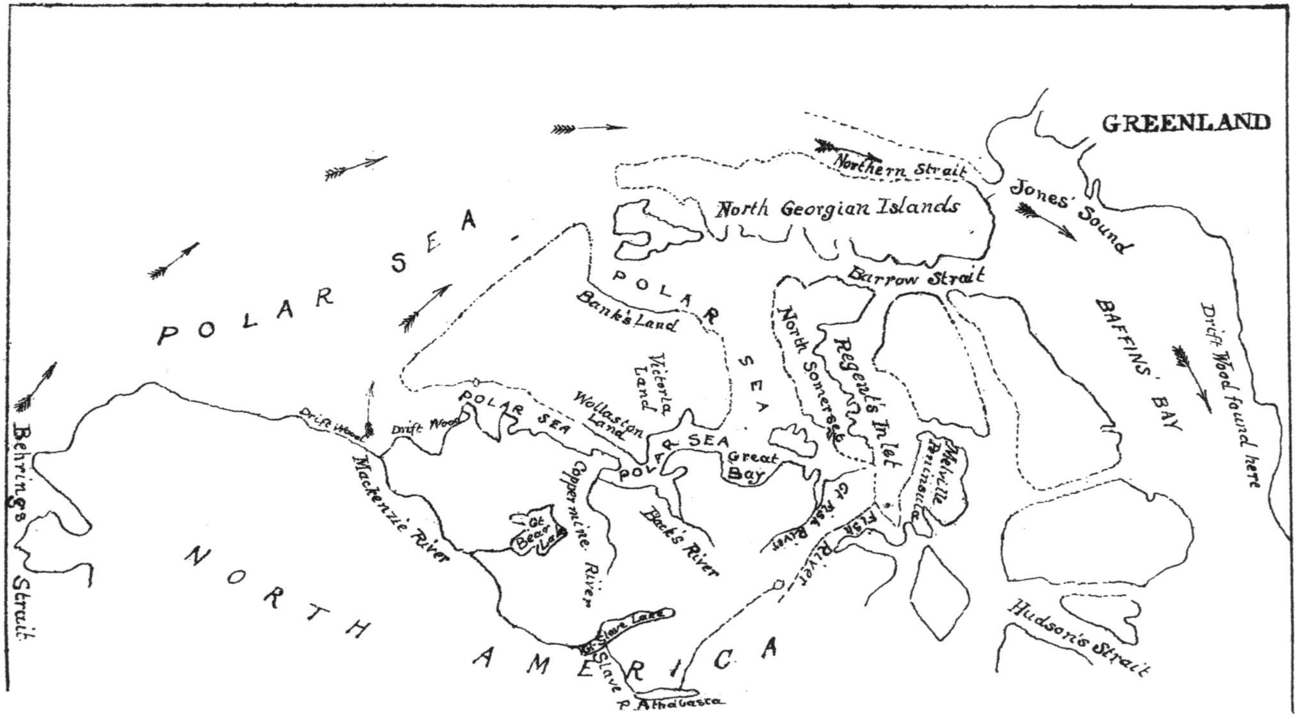

THE ADMIRALTY CHART 1854

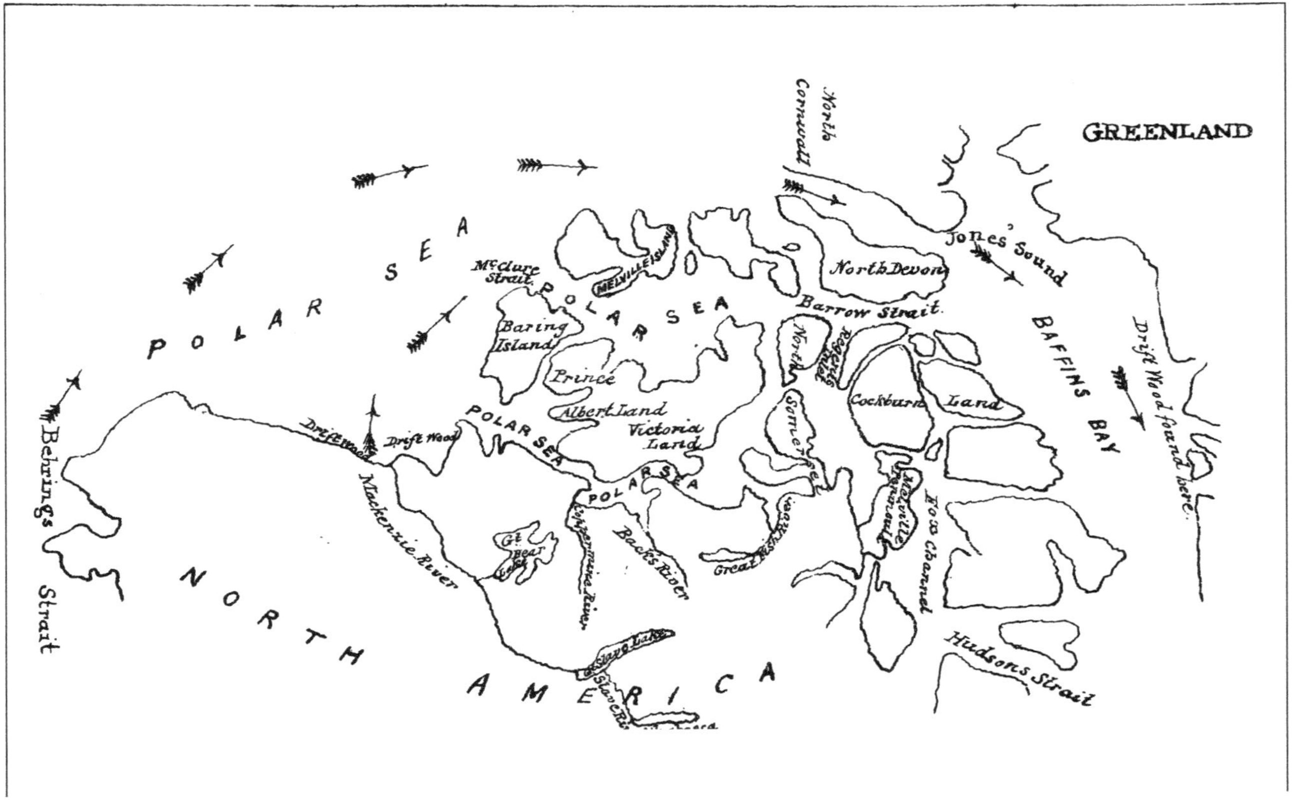
GREENLAND
North Cornwall
Jones' Sound
BAFFINS BAY
Drift Wood found here.
North Devon
Barrow Strait
POLAR SEA
Mc Clure Strait
MELVILLE ISLAND
Baring Island
Prince
Albert Land
Victoria Land
North
Somerset
Regents Inlet
Cockburn
Land
Melville Peninsula
Fox Channel
Hudsons Strait
POLAR SEA
POLAR SEA
POLAR SEA
Drift Wood
Drift Wood
Mackenzie River
Gt Bear Lake
Coppermine River
Backs River
Great Fish River
Slave Lake
Slave River
Behrings Strait
NORTH AMERICA

but not *more truthful* than the *Conjectural Chart* of 31 Jan. '45.

I have the honour to be,

Your faithful servant,

17, *Savile Row*, 27 *October*, '54. RICHARD KING.

POLAR SEA EXPEDITIONS AND POLAR LAND JOURNEYS.

To the Secretary to the Admiralty.

Sir,—The problem of a North Polar Passage between the Atlantic and Pacific Oceans having occupied your attention[49] for some years, I beg to submit to you a careful digest of the services which have taken place since you entered upon this field of research in 1818.

They are divisible into Polar Sea Expeditions and Polar Land Journeys. The Polar Sea Expeditions amount to ten, the Polar Land Journeys to three; seven out of the ten Polar Sea Expeditions may be briefly described;—Captain Lyon's Expedition was modestly called by him an "unsuccessful attempt to reach Repulse Bay;"

[49] Sir John Barrow was at this time Secretary to the Admiralty.

in the body of the narrative of Sir George Back's Expedition will be found the same tale which Captain Lyon told on his title-page; Sir John Ross returned after four years' wintering, without advancing a step towards the object in view; Sir Edward Parry failed in his attempt to reach the Polar Sea by Regent Inlet; Captain Beechy saw the Polar Sea, and that is all; and Captain Buchan was not so fortunate as Captain Beechy.

To the remaining three I call your particular attention. *First*,—To that of the Isabella of 385 tons and the Alexander of 252 tons, in command of Sir John Ross. Sir John Ross rounded Baffin Bay from East to West without discovering an opening to the West. *Second*,—To that of the Hecla of 375 tons and the Griper of 180 tons, in command of Sir Edward Parry with the same object in view as Sir John Ross. Instead of rounding Baffin Bay, Sir Edward Parry made an attempt to cross the Atlantic in the parallel of 58 deg, and afterwards in 73 deg. He succeeded, but the passage was one of great risk. The result of this

Expedition everybody knows and appreciates. We became acquainted with a Sea of 31 deg. of longitude, bounded on the North by broken land called the North Georgian Group, and on the South by Banks Land to the West, Land without a name to the East, and North Somerset between the two. The Sea between the Land without a name and North Somerset is called Regent Inlet, while that between North Somerset and Banks Land is without a name[50] *Third,*—To that of the Fury and Hecla in command of Sir Edward Parry, and fitted out with the view of reaching Regent Inlet by some unknown southern communication from Fox Channel. A communication was found, through the agency of the Esquimaux, in the Fury and Hecla Strait, but it was ice-clogged.

From these premises, what is the state of

[50] I shall shortly call the attention of the Government to the state of our geographical nomenclature, as a test how far the Admiralty can any longer be trusted with so important a function. If the Hydrographic Department were a second Sebastopol it must fall. I have "got shot enough in the locker" "*to smash*" (to use Sir C. Napier's admirable expression) that department.

things? "When you applied, in 1818, to " this question, the power of your vigorous " mind and penetrating judgment," a reflection was cast upon those who had hitherto laboured in this field of research, and no doubt was entertained that the problem would be speedily solved. But another expedition, and another, until they numbered ten, have sailed and returned, and the North-West Passage remains equally a problem; but with this difference, that it is no longer of a simple but of a compound character. The lands that have been brought to light are so many lesser puzzles, as additions to the Great Puzzle of three centuries.

The great difficulty in the way of these various attempts, all know, was ice, but no one, not even the author of the "Chrono- " logical History of Arctic Voyages[51]," has inquired, where was it found, where was it not found, and where was it for the future to be avoided. That which forced itself, especially upon Sir Edward Parry's mind, in his last expedition, was the fact of the adherence of ice to those shores

[51] Sir John Barrow.

which had an eastern aspect, while those of an opposite character were free. I have tested this fact in connection with the movements of all the Polar Sea Expeditions which have been set afloat since 1818, and I find that in every instance the difficulties arose from the same cause, the clinging to lands having an eastern aspect. It may be as well to mention them, for facts are always worth recording. Sir Edward Parry, in his second expedition, made attempts, for two successive summers, to penetrate the eastern entrance of Fury and Hecla Strait, and failed; and, in his third expedition, he lost the "Fury" while pushing his way along the eastern land of North Somerset. Sir John Ross, in his second expedition, was *four years advancing four miles* along the same eastern land, and was at last obliged to abandon his vessel. Captain Lyon and Sir George Back made, separately, unsuccessful attempts to reach Repulse Bay, which has an eastern aspect.

How, it may be inquired, is this general difficulty to be avoided? By doing, from experience, that which Baffin and Ross did from instinct, by taking the road, which is fairly open to us—the lands that have a western aspect. The difficulty then is clearly one of our own seeking, and no longer presents an insurmountable barrier to arctic research.

In 1818, you particularly called attention to the easterly current setting through Behring Strait in the Pacific, and the southerly current setting down Baffin Bay in the Atlantic, and you, in consequence, inferred that there must be a northern connecting sea to the two great oceans. It was, in fact, your most powerful if not your only lever to set in motion a Polar Sea Expedition. Yet the absence of a current in Lancaster Sound and the Fury and Hecla Strait never seems for a moment to have surprised you. By some unaccountable means you have been most effectually drawn from your original stronghold. It is quite clear that the master mind has not yet been at work on the subject of Polar Sea Expeditions, and while the polar travellers are divided among themselves and while you are intent upon Regent Inlet, which may, with as much justice be called Barrow His Hole as James Bay was called Gibbons His

Hole, and as the lower part of Regent Inlet would most assuredly have been called had Sir John Ross done as Sir John Barrow thinks he ought, Ross His Hole, the master mind is not likely to be brought to light.

And now let me call your attention to the other service which has been at work upon this interesting question. I mean the Polar Land Journeys, those fruitful missions but for which you would have been deprived of one or other of your favourite Polar Sea Expeditions. A short survey of the Polar Land Journeys will afford a standard of comparison with the Polar Sea Expeditions, and develope the true position. The publication of the travels of Hearne, the Fur Trader, for which we are indebted to a Frenchman[52], demonstrated that the Polar Sea could be reached overland by way of Canada, and the success which attended the first Government Journey proved that the opinion which had been formed was in every way correct. The distance between Coppermine River and Point Turnagain, as Sir John Franklin named the point of his retrograde movement, was thus made known to us. A

[52] La Perouse.

second journey added the distance between the Mackenzie and the Coppermine, and as far westward of the Mackenzie as Foggy Island, which far surpassed in extent the prosperous voyage of Sir Edward Parry in 1819 and 1820. A third expedition eclipsed all, and left to be surveyed but a small portion of the North American boundary of the Polar Sea; in that portion, small as it is, rests the problem of three centuries.

Is not this sufficient encouragement to send a fourth? The fruits of the *ten* Polar Sea Expeditions will not balance with those of *the last* of the three Polar Land Journeys; and the harvest of the first and the least successful of these interesting missions is greater than that which remains to be gathered, while in expenditure the three Land Journeys have certainly not cost more than two, if *one*, of the *ten* Polar Sea Expeditions. Even the little that has been done by the Polar Sea Expeditions is of a doubtful character. Banks Land, North Somerset, the North Georgian Group of Islands, and the boundaries of Barrow Strait are still problems; they are the lesser puzzles which I have mentioned. It is not so with the labours of Franklin, Richardson, and Simpson; the footing they made is permanent, while Croker Mountains[53] have dissolved, and islands threaten to be continents, and continents islands, the natural consequence of discovery in ships.

Had you advocated in favour of the Polar Land Journeys with a tithe of the zeal you have the Polar Sea Expeditions the North-West Passage would have long since ceased to be a problem, and, instead of a Baronetcy, you would deserve a Peerage, for the country would have been saved at least two hundred thousand pounds. But what use have you made of the Polar Land Journeys? You have invariably made use of them to stir up a Polar Sea Expedition, which, if it ceased not to exist in embryo,

[53] After Mr. Croker, Secretary to the Admiralty, afterwards named Barrow Strait, after Sir John Barrow, The original dispatch to the Admiralty had these words; "sailed over Croker Mountains, and called the place "Barrow Strait." This was a great *hit* of Sir Edward Parry to those who knew the antagonism existing between Sir John Barrow and Mr. Croker on the one hand, and Sir John Ross and Sir Edward Parry on the other.

as was the case with the expeditions under the command respectively of Captain Lyon, Captain Beechy, and Sir George Back, it had but a short uninteresting life. If you are really in earnest upon this subject, you have but one course to pursue; search for the truth, and value it when you find it. Another fruitless Polar Sea Expedition, and fruitless it will assuredly be, if not well digested, will be a lasting blot in the annals of our voyages of discovery[54].

I have the honour to be, Sir,

Your faithful servant,

17, *Savile Row*, 21 *December*, '44. RICHARD KING.

To the Secretary to the Admiralty.

Sir,—I revert to my letter of the 21st of December. The Polar Travellers are pretty well agreed as to the northern boundary of America from Behring Strait to Great Fish River Estuary. From this spot to Melville Peninsula, and to the north of this *hiatus*, all is conjecture. Such being the case, I venture an opinion that North

[54] And a fruitless Expedition it turned out.—It was commanded by Sir George Back, and designated "The ill-starred Voyage in the Terror."

Somerset is a part of the main continent of America[55], and that Victoria Land, Banks Land, and Wollaston Land, are portions of an extensive island, or an archipelago of islands[56], which, with the North Georgian Group, occupy a central position in the Polar Sea.

The Atlantic outlet of the Polar basin is thus divided. In other words, there are two North-West Passages. That between the oceanic group and the continent of America, which, at its eastern limit, is called Barrow Strait has alone been explored and is still incomplete[57]. A small sea-way remains to be discovered in the direction of Great Fish River Estuary. It will be found, I believe, washing the western shore of North Somerset. The Northern Strait, as I have named it for present convenience, has an outlet, in all probability, in Jones

[55] Subsequently established, and for which Sir John Ross obtained a "good service pension" of £.300 a-year.

[56] It has lately been determined that these *bits* of land, as they were when I wrote, are portions of an archipelago of islands occupying a central position in the Polar Sea.

[57] This also has proved correct, see Jones Sound, and Barrow Strait in chart.

Sound or hard by. Here we may look for the current which we lose at Behring Strait, and find in Baffin Bay. Here we may expect to discover a country teeming with life and its necessaries—man as well as beast, food as well as fuel. Thus much in conjecture. Now for the argument.

You implicitly believe North Somerset to be an island, and Fury and Hecla Strait to be the Atlantic outlet of the Polar Sea[58]. Where are the facts? A general assertion is very acceptable to mankind in general for life is too short for all to be equally attentive to one subject. But *seven* out of the *ten* Polar Sea Expeditions have failed since you entered upon this field of research in 1818, and the Admiralty, the newspapers inform us, after having solicited the Royal (not the Royal Geographical) Society for their opinion (sad mockery), are now urging Government to send the eleventh; a few facts then will be *apropos*[59]. They are, however, decidedly against you.

[58] "Royal Geographical Society's Journal," vol. vi, p. 35.

[59] I had it from high authority, after this letter was published, that Sir John Barrow solicited the Geogra-

Sir Edward Parry, who discovered Fury and Hecla Strait, and it has not been visited since his time, has distinctly stated there is no current in that Strait. Sir John Ross has published an Esquimaux chart of North Somerset wherein it is shewn to be a Peninsula. That you will say rests upon Indian information; it does, and so did the existence of the Polar Sea, Fury and Hecla Strait, Boothia Isthmus, and Melville Peninsula. And who doubts the accuracy of these Polar fishermen in these respects? On the contrary, their geographical knowledge is the admiration of the world. Are you, then, justified in doubting them in this solitary instance? The same woman—women are the geographers at the Pole—who figured that extraordinary isthmus, the Isthmus of Boothia, figured that land over which you are attempting to throw a doubt. When I contended this point in 1836, you referred to Sir George Back's decided opinion[60] of

phical Society in the first instance, and found them adverse.

[60] Back's Narrative, p. 408.

the termination of the eastern boundary of Great Fish River Estuary at Cape Hay, in which belief the gallant commander, to do honour to the Earl of Ripon the chief promoter of the Journey, named an island lying off the Cape, Ripon Island. Alas! Cape Hay has now lost its importance, and Ripon Island is not in existence. His lordship has no resting place at the Pole. Cape Britannia occupies the place of Ripon Island[61], and you are thus informed by that great traveller, Simpson, whose death all deplore, that I was right[62], and that Sir George Back was wrong. Sir John Ross was more careful of his patron, ex-sheriff Sir Felix Booth. He gave him six chances; 1, Boothia Felix; 2, Gulf of Boothia; 3, Isthmus of Boothia;

[61] Ripon Island, expunged from the chart in 1839, jumps up "Jim Crow" in 1854. The Admiralty *may*, from their inefficiency, lower England in the scale of nations, and they are fast doing it, and will succeed if that enduring animal, John Bull, lies much longer in a state of torpor, but they *shall not*, out of mere *bravado*, give existence to an island that does not exist.

[62] King's Narrative, vol. ii, p. 26.

4, Boothians; 5, Felix Harbour; 6, Sheriff's Harbour[63].

There is yet another important point which Simpson decided in my favour, which I mention as serving to put a value upon the conjectures I have ventured. The Great Bay discovered by Simpson in 1839 was supposed by me to exist in 1836[64], and which induced me to be so sanguine of success as to volunteer to the Secretary of State for the Colonies for the time being, year after year, to conduct a journey such as Simpson undertook and successfully carried out[65]; for, if several jutting points of land had occupied the space of that bay, not one season but several seasons would have been required for its survey.

[63] Sir Felix Booth was sheriff of London at the period of the discovery.

[64] King's Narrative, vol. ii, p. 77.

[65] The Hudson Bay Company received from the British Government, as a reward for adopting my plan of a Polar Land Journey—which was pre-eminently successful—and as a *sop in the pan* for eclipsing *their* Polar Sea Expedition—which was pre-eminently unsuccessful—and entitled the "Ill starred voyage in the Terror,"—a baronetcy for their chairman, Sir John Henry Pelly, and a knighthood for their manager, Sir George Simpson.

A few words in conclusion regarding the Northern Strait. It is well known that the current setting down Baffin Bay brings drift wood with it, and it is equally well known that no drift wood passes through Fury and Hecla, Hudson, and Barrow Straits. The presumptive evidence is very convincing to my mind that a large portion of the wood which is drifted down Mackenzie River is carried out to sea, and, catching the western termination of the oceanic group I have mentioned, is rolled onwards by the Polar current until it finds its exit, losing in quantity as it travels, in Baffin Bay by Jones Sound[66]. Additionally, the Esquimaux of Hudson Strait and of the Mackenzie River are, in manners and customs, alike[67]; the intermediate tribes altogether different. The Ethnologist would infer, if the natives of Hudson Strait had found their way from Mackenzie River along the coast of North America, that they would have lost, in the years that must have been spent in this migration and in the intermar-

[66] This Polar Passage is now a matter of fact.

[67] A paper in the Journal of the Ethnological Society of London, by Dr. King, M.D.

riages that must have taken place, somewhat in manners and customs, and that consequently they had followed another route, and the most likely route is that of the drift wood. I cannot but believe that many members of the Esquimaux family remain to be discovered, and that they will be found lining the shores of the supposed Northern Strait.

Now, let me not be misunderstood. Although I am contending for a Polar Land Journey, I am by no means desirous of putting a stop to the Polar Sea Expedition, which it appears Government has under its consideration. Let them sail and prosper if they can; I only wish to point out what seems to me, after mature study, to be the right path. I am no economist, but if thousands of pounds are to be spent let us have a good investment; and the only safe investment in my opinion is in a Polar Land Journey. In a third letter I shall submit a plan for the discovery of the North-west Passage, or rather the North-west Passages, by a Polar Land Journey. It is a source of deep regret that I am obliged thus publicly to address you, but it is my only hope of obtaining a hearing, seeing that since 1836

I have incessantly been labouring in vain to that end. I am the better able to do this now than formerly, because the reflection can no longer be cast upon me "that it is from interested motives and not "from a love of science."

I have the honour to be Sir,

Your faithful servant,

17, *Savile Row*, 8 *Jan.*, '45. RICHARD KING.

To the Secretary to the Admiralty.

SIR,—In submitting a plan for the exploration of the northern coast of North America, and the islands adjacent, I scarcely know where to begin, for if I consider the explorers at once at their starting point in the heart of the country I shall have Sir John Franklin, as in 1836, calling it "meagre[68];" and if I minutely describe the inward route I shall merit the charge of making a long story. Conciseness in conducting a Polar Journey, and in reporting it, is so essential to the traveller that I prefer to come under Sir John Franklin's lash; and, by anticipation, refer him to his own narrative or to that of Sir Alexander Mackenzie for a

[68] See Annals of Philosophy.

minute description of the well-known route from Montreal to Athabasca.

I propose that a party of two officers—one being of the medical profession—a boat carpenter, and 13 men fully equipped for the service, should leave Montreal in Canada sufficiently early to reach the Athabasca Lake in July. Here half the baggage should be left, and the boat carpenter and two men should remain, in order to build a boat 28 feet long, an occupation of three weeks. The explorers should then proceed to the head waters of the Fish River to fix upon an eligible position to winter, and the inner man as well as the outer man should be taken into consideration. The route to the Fish River from the Athabasca Lake is well known to the Indians and Fur Traders, and is minutely described in "King's "Journey to the Polar Sea by Great "Fish River." One officer and five men, with an Indian guide, should then return to the Athabasca Lake, and, having despatched the boat carpenter with the Indian guide and the two men to the Fish River party, there to build a second boat, proceed in the newly-built boat, *viâ* the Slave and

Mackenzie Rivers, to Great Bear Lake to winter.

The parties, which, for convenience, it will be as well to call the eastern and western party, having securely housed themselves, should at once adapt their means to their ends, in getting through the winter and providing for the future, for which purpose I refer them to the narratives of Sir Alexander Mackenzie and Sir John Franklin; but as the authors saw things differently, and met, in consequence, with feasting or famine, success or failure, the exercise of some judgment will be required in the reference. To collect and hoard provision, and to pave the way to the Polar Sea, so as to be on its shores as early as the navigation will permit, and to observe all and everything in the vast field before them, are the main features of an Arctic winter with a land party. With a sea party, such as the Admiralty have proposed, the time will be spent in acting plays and other merry-andrew tricks that the officers may make a book out of the sterility around them.

The western party will be further occupied in transporting, as the traveller Simpson, their boat to Coppermine River, and the eastern party their boat to Great Fish River. As soon as these rivers are open the parties must be in progress, the one for Cape Britannia, or Ripon Island as it was once called, and the other for Victoria Land; the one to ascertain the connection of the mainland with that of North Somerset, or with Melville Peninsula, and, if the former, the character of its western shore; and the other to trace Victoria Land westerly with the view of testing its value relatively to the North-West-Passage.

If I am rightly informed, the Hudson Bay Company have already despatched one of their clerks, Mr. Rae, on an overland journey, for the purpose of making the survey which I propose for the eastern party. This is an interesting fact, if true, but it by no means sets aside the necessity for a Polar Land Journey; for, on the arrival of the explorers at the Athabasca, if it should be found that Mr. Rae has been wholly successful, then, instead of one, two boats should be built there, and the parties, instead of separating, should winter together at Great Bear Lake; and, on reaching Victoria Land, turn the prows of their boats east and west, so as to double the power employed in solving the great problem in that direction. To enter further into detail is unnecessary until the service is determined upon, but in order that my ability to supply the minutest detail may not be questioned I take leave to state that I led the mission in search of Sir John Ross not only *into* but *out of* the Polar Regions.

In Queen Elizabeth's time the North-West Passage problem was considered of sufficient importance to demand the attention of commissioners expressly appointed. If Queen Victoria will follow the steps of Queen Elizabeth I will undertake to prove the practicability of the plan here proposed, and the impracticability of the plan proposed by the Admiralty. The first report that reached England of the last of the Polar Sea Expeditions led the Admiralty "to "auger favourably of its success." I augured differently, and published my auguration. It was subsequently designated the "Ill-starred voyage in the Terror[69]."

It has been considered essential to have the cordial co-operation of the Hudson

[69] In command of Sir George Back.

Bay Company in all overland journeys. I do not know whether the Admiralty have consulted the Royal Society upon this point, but I am prepared to prove, if the commander of an overland journey such as I propose should entirely depend upon the co-operation of the company, he is wholly unfit for the command[70]. It may even be thought satisfactory to find the Hudson Bay Company at last endeavouring to fulfil the engagement they entered into in obtaining their[71] charter as a Fur Company, that

[70] Sir George Simpson sent to Mr. Anderson, who lately descended Great Fish River, three Iroquois, and but for them, he says, he could not have mastered that impetuous stream. Of course not; it was Iroquois I intended to take, and thus to be entirely independent of the Company.

[71] "Whereas our dear entirely beloved cousin, Prince Rupert, &c. &c., have, at their own great cost and charges, undertaken an expedition for Hudson Bay, in the N.W. parts of America for the discovery of a new passage into the South Sea. * * * And whereas the said undertakers for their further encouragement in the said design have humbly besought us to incorporate them, and grant unto them and their successors the whole trade and commerce of all those seas, straits, and bays, rivers, lakes, creeks, and sounds, in whatsoever

of prosecuting by all possible means the North-West Passage; but effectually as they have hitherto closed their Country to the man of science, it cannot last much longer. Geographical science is surely not all that requires furthering in North America. We have to thank the Admiralty and the Hudson Bay Company for a state of ignorance regarding that Country, which, in comparison with what has been learned of Northern Asia by Russia, places us nationally in a most disadvantageous light.

I have the honour to be,

Your faithful servant,

17, *Savile Row*, 31 *Jan.*, '45. RICHARD KING.

Sir John Barrow hated me at once and for ever for having thus pointed out the manifest incompleteness of his Polar schemes. He vowed he would smash the impudent fellow who presumed to differ with him on a subject he flattered himself was exclusively his own; but the materials he had to deal with were not so easily annihilated. "With the greedy perseverance of

latitude they shall be, that lie within the entrance of the straits commonly called Hudson Straits, &c. &c."

" the gamester, who feels an intimate per-
" suasion that if he could only hold out for
" one more trial, fortune would turn to the
" red[72]," Sir John Barrow tried yet once more; and *the eleventh* naval expedition was resolved upon, in command of Sir George Back.

Sir John Barrow must have been a cock-fighter in his day, hence his disposition to *pit* one animal against another; for instance, Parry *v.* Ross, Ross *v.* Ross[73], Back *v.* King[74]. Sir John Barrow was not physiognomist enough to play so desperate a game, so he lost on every *pit*, and then completed his Polar insolvency by persuading Franklin to go and form the *nucleus* of an *iceberg*[75]; a man who had highly distinguished himself in the conduct of Polar

[72] *Times*, 1 Feb. '56.

[73] Uncle and Nephew —A nice *hash* Sir John Barrow made of these animals—they have not yet done fighting, although the cock-pit itself is a " by-gone."

[74] This cock-fighting affair will scarcely be intelligible to those who have not made Polar matters their study.

[75] I told Sir John Barrow publicly at the time Franklin sailed that he was sending him to form the *nucleus* of an *iceberg*.

Land Journeys, and was consequently wholly unfitted for Polar Sea Expeditions.

Young Admiralty, in the form of "Blue "Jacket," take warning from me, for I should have been smashed over and over again, if, in dealing with the *North Pole*, I had been dealing with *my daily bread*. Be particularly *ignorant* in all your dealings with Sir Maurice F. F. Berkley, M.P., for the Board of Admiralty in these days is as much *his Board* as the Board of Admiralty in Sir John Barrow's days was *his Board*. In Sir Maurice F. F. Berkley, M.P., you have the counterpart of Sir John Barrow, with this vast difference, that he is entirely deficient in those qualifications which rendered Sir John Barrow the great man. Sir John Barrow possessed strong affections and high talents and acquirements, and could *love* and *hate*, while Sir Maurice F. F. Berkley, M.P., can only *hate* and *hate*.

Now mark, on the 26th October, '54, I informed the Admiralty I was preparing a plan to be submitted to them in search of The Franklin Remains; that was on a Wednesday. On the following Tuesday morning this letter in real print in the

Times appeared to my astonished eyes, signed John Rae, Tavistock Hotel, Oct. 30.

Dr. Rae made a sad mess of *himself in* writing two different accounts of his "*relics*," and now he makes a sad mess of the *Admiralty* in publishing *this letter*. He states—" It may interest your readers to " learn that two overland journeys have " been decided upon—the one, in boats to " go down the Mackenzie River, in search " of Captain Collinson, the other, in canoes " down Great Fish River, to make further " inquiry into the fate of Sir John Franklin's " people, and to endeavour to obtain some " more relics, and should any of the remains " be found, to place them decently under " ground. About noon on Friday, it was " arranged by the Lord's Commissioners of " the Admiralty that these expeditions " should be left wholly in the hands of the " Hudson Bay Company[76]."

Then let Sir James Graham excuse himself if he can for writing me, on the Saturday, one of the stereotyped letters of the Admiralty, *merely acknowledging* the receipt

[76] *Times*, 31 Oct., '55.

of my letter of the 26th October, '54. The common feelings of a gentleman should surely have dictated to him the propriety of informing me of his proceedings on the Friday, and thus have spared me the labour of studying my plan until I was cut short by Dr. Rae's letter in the *Times.*

And now to the next step of my little history. On the 20th June, '55, Mr. James Anderson, a chief factor in the service of the Hudson Bay Company, started from Fort Resolution, a trading Post of the Company on the Great Slave Lake, for Montreal Island and Point Ogle, in three canoes, and returned on the 17th September. This is the narrative ;—

" We had the advantage of Sir George Back's Map and Narrative, the former, the one attached to his book, was on far too small a scale for our purpose, but the latter was of great service. We found the want also of an Esquimaux interpreter[77].

---

[77] No map—no interpreter—and strangers in the land of their search!!! Sir George Back's expedition is known as " *The ill-" starred Voyage in the Terror.*" The Hudson Bay Company's journey will be known as " *The ill-conceived Search for Franklin.*"

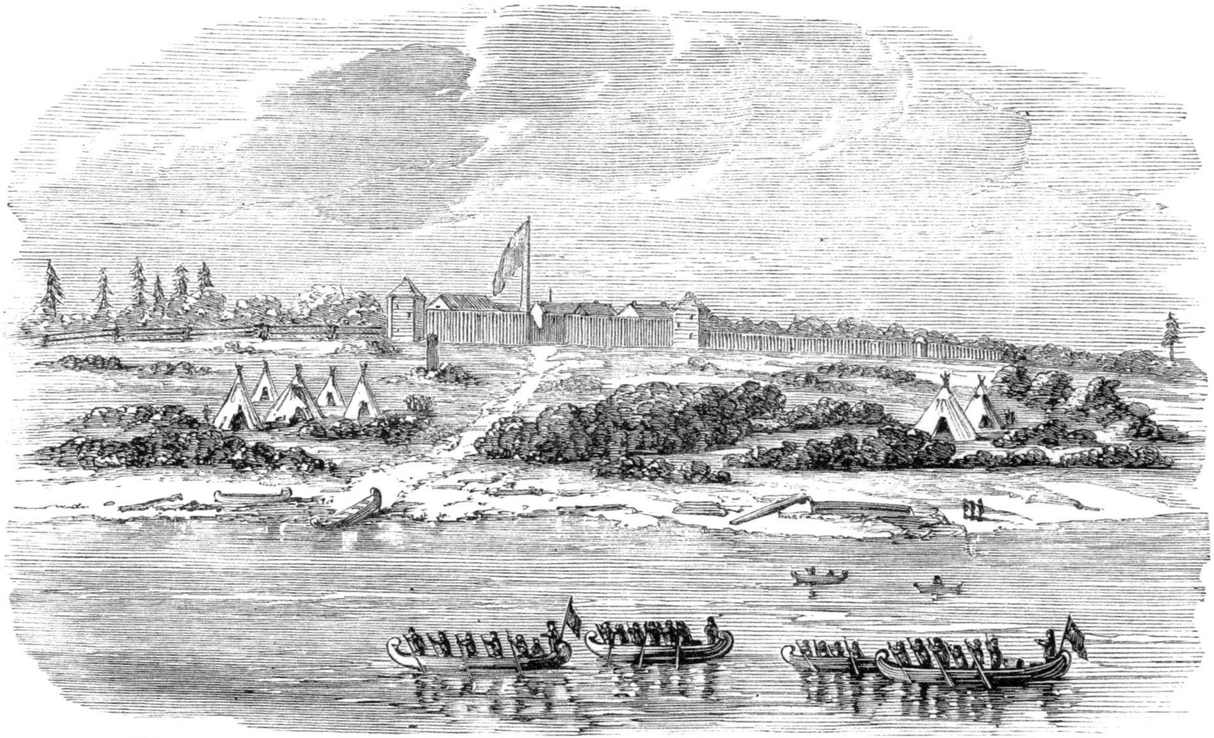

POLAR LAND JOURNEY BY GREAT FISH RIVER FOR THE REMAINS OF THE FRANKLIN EXPEDITION

Starting from Fort Resolution, Great Slave Lake.

" On the 30th July, '55, at the rapids below Lake Franklin, three Esquimaux lodges were seen on the opposite shore, and shortly after an elderly man crossed to us. After the portage was made, we crossed over, and immediately perceived various articles belonging to a boat, such as tent poles and kayack paddles made out of ash oars, pieces of mahogany, elm, oak, and pine; also copper and sheet iron boilers, tin soup tureens, pieces of instruments, a letter nip with the date 1843, a broken hand saw, chisels, &c. Only one man was at the lodges, but the women, who were very intelligent, made us understand by words and signs, that these articles came from a boat, and the white men belonging to it had died of starvation.

" We, of course, by shewing them books and written papers, endeavoured to ascertain if they possessed any papers, offering to give them plenty of the goods we had with us for them; but, though they evidently understood us, they said they had none. They did not scruple to shew us all their hidden treasures. Besides the man, there were three women and eight children. The remainder of the party, two men and three lads, were seen towards evening.

" Point Beaufort was reached on the 31st. We were detained there the next day till half-past two p.m. by a S.W. gale. We then took the traverse to Montreal Island. To seaward the ice appeared perfectly firm and unbroken.

" When about three miles from the Island, a large stream of ice was observed coming at a great rate before the wind and tide out of Elliott Bay and the other deep Bays to the westward. Every sinew was strained to reach the land; but we were soon surrounded by ice, and for some time were in most imminent danger. The ice was from six to seven feet thick, perfectly sound, and drifting at the rate of five or six miles an hour. In fifteen minutes after we had passed, the whole Channel to Point Beaufort was choked with ice. Had we not succeeded in crossing on this day, we should have been detained on the eastern shore till the 10th.

"We had thus arrived at the first spot indicated by my instructions. The next two days were devoted by the entire party to the examination of the Island, and the small Islands in its vicinity. On a high ridge of rocks, at the South-east point of the Island, a number of Esquimaux caches were found, and, besides seal oil, various articles were found belonging to a boat or ship; such as chain hooks, chisels, blacksmith's shovel and cold chisel, tin oval boiler, a bar of unwrought iron about three feet long, one and a-half inch broad, and a quarter of an inch thick; small pieces of rope, bunting, and a number of sticks strung together, on one of which was cut 'Mr. Stanley (Surgeon of Erebus).' A little lower down was a large quantity of chips, shavings, and ends of plank of pine, elm, ash, oak, and mahogany, evidently sawed by unskilful hands; every chip was turned over, and on one of them was found the word 'Terror' carved. It was evident that this was the spot where the boat was cut up by the Esquimaux. Not even a scrap of paper could be discovered, and though rewards were offered, and the most minute search made over the whole Island, not a vestige of the remains of our unfortunate countrymen could be discovered.

" On the 5th August, '55, we succeeded in crossing over to the western mainland, opposite to Montreal Island, and the whole party was employed in making a most minute search as far as the point of Elliott Bay, and also to the northward. The whole Coast between Montreal Island and Point Pechel was searched by a land party, always accompanied by Mr. Stewart or myself. Many very old Esquimaux encampments were seen, but not a trace of the party.

" Early on the 7th August, '55, the entire party, with the exception of two of the Iroquois, who were left to repair the canoes, started in light marching trim, taking the Halket boat with us. Five men followed all the sinuosities of the coast, while the others were spread at equal distances inland, Mr. Stewart and myself taking the middle space. Shortly after leaving the encampment a river was forded ; this must be a large stream at a high stage of water. It was called Lemisieurier River, after a relative of Mr. Stewart's. No fuel was found in our encampments, and in two hours we left all signs of vegetation behind. The remainder of the Peninsula is composed of high sandhills intersected by deep valleys, evidently overflowed at spring tides and during gales.

" We encamped late opposite Maconochie Island, and the only vestige of the missing party found was a small piece of cod-line, and a strip of striped cotton about two inches long and an inch broad. These were found at Point Ogle, in an Esquimaux encampment of perhaps three or four years of age.

"Next morning a piece of open water enabled us to launch the Halket boat, and explore Maconochie Island, but nothing was found. It was impossible to cross over to Point Richardson, as I wished, the ice driving through the strait between it and Maconochie Island at a fearful rate. About three o'clock in the afternoon we began to retrace our steps through a tremendous storm of wind and rain. It may be thought strange that the remains of so large a party could not be discovered. It is my opinion that a party in a starving condition would have chosen a low spot, where they could haul their boat up and have had some shelter; and that, if they perished there, their bones have been long since covered by sand or gravel forced up by the ice[78]. Any books or papers left open would be destroyed by the perpetual winds and rain in this quarter in a very short space of time; for instance, a large book, *Raper's Navigation*, was left open on a cloak at Montreal Island; it was blown open, and the leaves were pattering about in such a way that, had it not been instantly closed, it would soon have been torn in pieces.

"JAMES ANDERSON, C.F."

---

[78] This notion is far too absurd to be entertained. Besides it does not account for the absence of all remains of the five that died at Montreal Island.

The Examiner notices this journey with its all-powerful pen.

" All that is ever likely to be told us of the closing scene of the great tragedy which ends the history of Arctic exploration, we now know. It is now absolutely certain that, had attention been paid to the representations and entreaties of Dr. King, persisted in by him so early as 1847, search would then have been made in the right direction, and there would still have been a chance for the survivors who in 1850 reached the coast at the mouth of the Great Fish River—to die.

" Dr. Rae had understood the Esquimaux to mean Montreal Island, and Point Ogle near it, as the places where the white men perished in 1850. The recent search has determined the locality beyond dispute. After a day or two of unsuccessful exploration, one of the first relics found was a part of one of the boats of the Terror, with the name of that vessel branded on it. The Esquimaux said that some tribes further north had seen the ships, and knew them to have been crushed by the ice,—knew them to have met probably in Victoria Straits, in 1848, with that accident which many former voyagers are known to have been often within but a hair's breadth of escaping. Here too was a fragment of a boat, to tell how far, after suffering and toil, at least one band of men escaping from the vessels had advanced its efforts to reach to some one of the northern stations of the Hudson Bay Company. There was found also on Montreal Island another fragment of this boat, on which the name of Sir John Franklin was carved. There was found besides part of a snow-shoe, known to be of English manufacture, 'being made of 'oak, a species of wood which no man accustomed to 'use such shoes would ever select for the purpose;' and upon it the name of Mr. Stanley, surgeon to Franklin's own ship the Erebus, was carved. There was also a ship's hammer; there were oars, boat-kettles, empty meat cases; there were remains of a flag; and there was a letter-clip. But there were no papers, and no bones of the men who died.

"Here, then, it was that in the winter of 1850 the survivors of the Erebus and Terror ran their boats upon the beach, and, too weak to proceed further, crawled ashore to die. It was in the same part of the world that Franklin, thirty years before, had suffered all the famine man can suffer and yet live. By the Copper Mine River he had eaten *tripe de roche*, and supped on scraps of roasted leather. By the estuary of Great Fish River, if he was among those who came so far in the direction of man's help, he died.

"One of the lost crew, the Esquimaux relates, died on Montreal Island, the rest perished on the coast of the mainland. 'The wolves were very thick.' Only one white man seems to have been living when their tribe arrived, and him it was too late to save. An Esquimaux woman saw him die. 'He was large and strong,' she said, 'and sat on the sandy beach, his head resting 'on his hands, and thus he died.' A death that shall not be forgotten by the poets, in days hereafter[79]."

---

[79] *Examiner*, 12 Jan. '56.

What a sad destiny was Franklin's. Sir James Ross "could not conceive any position in which he could be placed from which he would make for Great Fish River;" and Sir John Richardson "did not think, under any circumstances, he would attempt that route;" and yet these officers were selected to be the leaders of a searching party, the one by sea and the other by land, the one having his starting point at Barrow Strait, and the other at Mackenzie River, with instructions to meet, so as to cross the estuary of Great Fish River; to attract, in fact, each other. This was not possible, seeing how they were *charged*, and, as might have been expected, at a given point they *repelled* each other, and thus *tabooed* The Franklin Expedition—to death.

If this combined effort by sea and by land had comprised a larger area,—if the descent of Coppermine, Great Fish, and Mackenzie Rivers had been made at one and the same time, and each party, on making the Polar Sea, had been instructed to cross over to Victoria Land, and then to trace that land, as Thomas Simpson traced it, in the direction of North Somerset, it would have comprised a plan in accordance with the meanest capacity, and completely *netted* the lost adventurers; but to imagine for one moment that two men should meet, the starting points being Barrow Strait on the one hand, and Mackenzie River on the other, displayed a state of ignorance of Polar difficulty that reflects no credit on those who planned it, nor on those who undertook to conduct it.

To have entertained anything half so preposterous, especially when life and death on a large scale was *the stake*,—was an utter recklessness such as the Admiralty alone was capable of. Thomas Simpson started, not from the Mackenzie but from the Coppermine, and he had three of my best men with him,—Mackay, Sinclair, and Taylor,—and yet the known physical power and endurance of that extraordinary man barely enabled him to reach Great Fish River. These are his words, written in indellible characters on the spot—*no cooking*, for this great man died on his journey, with his manuscript in hand.—"The survey of the land of North "Somerset, which was the main object of

" the Terror's ill-starred Voyage, would " necessarily demand the whole time and " energies of another Expedition, having a " starting point much nearer to the scene " of operations than Coppermine River[80]."

It is a weak point in Sir John Richardson's character not to have insisted, as the old friend of Sir John Franklin, upon the combination of search I suggested. Even if Sir John Richardson were strong in the belief that Sir John Franklin was not to be found at Great Fish River, he should have shewn himself the scientific man and the great man, and encouraged my plan, were it only for science' sake.

It was not thought possible that Sir John Richardson and Sir James Ross could do otherwise than meet. Then how was it they did not? Because they *could not* and *would not.* Sir John Richardson could not, because he was too old. I told him so; I

[80] *Times*, 18 April, '40. I quote the Times in preference to the published works, because I like first impressions. Sir George Back's Narrative and Map were so *over-cooked* that I lost all knowledge of the *raw material.* Sir John Barrow made a sad *hash* of Back as well as the Ross'.

told Lord Grey so[81]; others said so. Sir James Ross *would not,* because he had resolved to turn his *errand of mercy* into an *errand of self-aggrandisement.* Sir John Ross told Lord Auckland so[82]; everybody knew so. And it is AGONY to reflect, when these officers broke down, that they stood face to face at the very threshold of the whereabouts of their old friend[83].

Then comes the Hudson Bay Company Expedition, dispatched to bury the bodies and ascertain their sad history, and what becomes of it? The man who had pointed out Montreal Island and Point Ogle as the death-spot of The Franklin Expedition, and was intimately acquainted with the locality,

[81] *Vide* p. 47.

[82] *Vide* p. 73.

[83] Sir George Back settled the vexed question in language peculiarly his own. "He *wholly* rejected *all* " and *every* idea of *any* attempt on the part of Franklin " to send boats to *any* point of the mainland in the " vicinity of Great Fish River[1]." As Medical Referee to the London and Continental Life Office, I have to read language of this kind:—Are you sober? Particularly so; a mere mistake, I generally find, for Particularly drunk.

[1] *Vide* p. 88.

was not to go and bury the bodies and fetch the little history they had bequeathed to their country,—the last message each had delivered to his nearest and dearest relative or friend.

The nation, with one voice, would most assuredly have awarded to him that honour, but that Sir James Graham, with all haste, knowing well the *little bit of active mortality* he had to deal with, flung him aside, and with him such men as Osborne, Pim, and M'Cormick, before he had an opportunity to appeal to his nation.

What a sad destiny was Franklin's; it extended even to his very remains. Sir James Graham, upon whom fell the duty of providing for the decent burial of these remains, instead of performing this office, which better blood than himself would have esteemed an honour of no little account, delegated that office to a commercial company, notoriously ignorant[84] of all things except rat skins and cat skins[85], utterly

[84] Science and Commerce never yet went hand in hand.

[85] The sable is sometimes called sable-cat;—and musk-rat is the ordinary name of the musquash or lesser

indifferent as to the mode in which they performed the task.

He had no right to do this. He had no right to hand over the bodies of 138 gallant sailors to a commercial company. He had no right to give them any other funeral than that due to them, as belonging to Her Majesty's Service. He surely should have dispatched an officer of Her Majesty's Service, of known ability, to perform that office, and to place a monument over their grave. He has compromised the nation in having thus neglected his duty.

But Dr. King was not the man to go, because he would find bodies at Montreal Island and Point Ogle whether or no. No such thing, Sir James Graham. No such thing, Sir Maurice F. F Berkeley, M.P. It is *as old as Adam*, that is to say, *North Pole Adam*, that I have always *bargained* I would have as my companion an officer of Her Majesty's Service, selected and appointed by the Government. I was *too old a soldier*,

beaver,—the little animal which supplied us with beaver hats before silk hats came into use.—*King's Narrative*, vol. i. p. 115.

even as far back as 1847, not to see the importance of having *a living witness* to every transaction of my journey[86].

Now what has come of the Commercial Company's Expedition to bury the remains of Franklin and to learn his sad history? They reach Point Ogle and Montreal Island. They find undoubted evidence of the truth of the Esquimaux accounts, and they are content with collecting a few relics to add to Dr. Rae's relics, and return. They never search King Cache of Montreal Island,—because they had no map,—because they had not read the Narrative of Thomas Simpson,—because they had selected a crew who were utter strangers in the land.

They do not ask of the Esquimaux the particulars of the Franklin tragedy—because they could not speak to them,—because they had no interpreter. They did not mark the spot where forty of their countrymen met their death,—because they had not provided themselves with a simple monument of granite. They do not seek for the history, in writing, of their sad fate in the only spot it was likely to be found,—

[86] *Vide* p. 25.

because they had never heard that such a spot had existence. *O tempora! O mores!*

With these feelings I addressed the humble prayer which concludes this narrative to the Lords Commissioners of the Admiralty, which I now address to my country at large, in whose hands now rests The Fate of The Franklin Expedition.

To the Right Honourable The Lords Commissioners of the Admiralty.

My Lords,—Your Lordships are aware that, in the years 1833—35, I was the Medical Officer attached to the Polar Land Journey in search of Sir John Ross, and that, for a considerable period, I commanded the party.

The knowledge which I acquired in that Journey, joined to an anxious desire for the advancement of Geographical science, led me to investigate the causes of the failure of former expeditions, having for their object the discovery of the North-West Passage, and to entertain views as to the means of solving that problem, which were, at that time, at variance with the opinions held by other Arctic travellers, although their soundness has since been established by the discoveries of Sir Robert M'Clure, Sir Edward Belcher, Mr. Thomas Simpson, and others.

In February 1845, when it had been determined by your Lordships to despatch Sir John Franklin, with the Erebus and Terror, to prosecute the discovery of the "Passage" from Barrow Strait, I pressed upon Her Majesty's Government, although without success, the expediency of aiding the search by means of a Polar Land Journey down the Coppermine and Great Fish Rivers.

In 1847, after a lapse of two years since tidings had been received of the Erebus and Terror, doubts were entertained as to their safety; and on the 10th of June in that year, I submitted to the Government a statement of the grounds which led me to the conviction that the position of the lost Expedition was on the western land of North Somerset, and I proposed to communicate with and convey succour to them by means of a Land Journey down Great Fish River.

My proposal, however, was not entertained; on the contrary, two Naval expeditions were despatched, one from each end of the Continent, and a party was charged with a Land Journey for the purpose of searching the Coast, not in the locality which I had pointed out, but between the Mackenzie and Coppermine Rivers.

It is unnecessary for me to dilate upon the fruitless result of these expeditions. On their return, the sympathies of the whole world were aroused to the fate of The Franklin Expedition, and a fleet of vessels was despatched, partly by the State, and partly by private enterprise, in search of the missing navigators; but most unfortunately the coast near the mouth of Great Fish River was again omitted from the search. For the third time I pressed upon the Government the expediency of a Land Journey, for the purpose of examining this neglected spot; and, in a letter addressed to your Lordships, on the 18th of February, 1850, in which I used the prophetic words,—"The route of Great "Fish River will sooner or later be under-"taken in search of Sir John Franklin,"

I repeated the offer I had previously made, to lead a party in the search.

Your Lordships, however, acting upon the advice of the recently appointed Arctic Council, who, to use the words of one of its members,—" did not think that, under " any circumstances, Franklin would at- " tempt the route of Great Fish River," ignored my plan, and declined my services, and despatched a further Naval Expedition, the crews of which returned from a fruitless search, after the unparalleled desertion of no less than five vessels. Their journey, however, was not altogether without result, for although they failed to find or save the missing navigators, they discovered the long-sought " Passage," in the identical position, it may be observed, laid down in an imaginary Chart which I had published some years previously, and had upheld against the opinion of other travellers up to the period of the discovery.

In 1854 Dr. Rae was despatched by the Hudson Bay Company to complete a survey of the West coast of Boothia; and, although he informed the public, in his letter addressed to the " Times," on the 11th of

December, 1852, " that there was not the " slightest hope of finding any traces of the " lost navigators in the quarter to which he " was going," yet, strange as it may have appeared to him, he ascertained from the Esquimaux, on arriving in Pelly Bay, that about forty white men had perished four years previously at Montreal Island, and on the banks of Great Fish River;—in the *very spot*, I may observe, where Dr. Rae and the Arctic Council had come to the conclusion that the lost navigators could by no human possibility be found; and in the *identical locality* which I had never ceased to urge was the precise point which Franklin would endeavour to reach, and where traces of the expedition would infallibly be found.

At the time of receiving this intelligence Dr. Rae was at a distance of about 100 miles from Point Ogle; and it appears, from his official Report to the Hudson Bay Company, that he subsequently arrived at Castor and Pollux River, which is scarcely forty-five miles distant from that spot, and that, instead of hastening forward to verify or disprove the horrible story of cannibalism and death, related to him by the Esquimaux, he turned aside at a right angle, and travelled not less than double that distance, in a northerly direction, up to Cape Porter!

Without pausing to inquire the reason which induced Dr. Rae to turn aside, when he was within forty-five miles from a spot in which so much horrible interest was centred, and when he must have been well aware that neither the Government nor the people of England would rest satisfied until the locality of the reputed tragedy should have been examined;—without pausing, I say, to advert to this inexplicable proceeding on his part, I hasten to remind your Lordships that the accounts thus brought home by Dr. Rae, at once proved the incontestible accuracy of the views which I had so long and unsuccessfully pressed upon the attention of Her Majesty's Government, respecting the locality in which some traces or tidings of Franklin would be found.

In the following year the soundness of my views was at length tacitly admitted, by the despatch of an expedition, in canoes, down Great Fish River, almost in the precise manner which I had so vainly advocated in 1845, 1847, 1848, and again in 1850: and, from the official Report of Mr. Anderson, the leader of that expedition, (published in the "Times" of the 11th instant), it appears that, on the banks of that river, and on Montreal Island, some slight traces of the missing navigators have been found.

It is useless now to inquire what would have been the result if your Lordships had acceded to my earnest and repeated entreaties, and permitted me, in 1847 or 1848, to lead an expedition to the spot where these sad relics have since been found; no doubt can, I think, exist in the mind of any reasoning being, that, if those entreaties had been acceded to, a portion, at least, of the lost expedition would, at the present moment, be alive, and in England.

It is not with any view to my own aggrandisement, or with any feeling of self-laudation, that I submit this hurried analysis of the recent Arctic Expeditions to your Lordships' consideration. If such were my object, I should point out further instances in which the discoveries of Simpson and others have proved the accuracy of my views respecting the conformation of the Polar Regions. But I think it right to place on record a statement, however hasty and incomplete, shewing the correctness of the opinion which I so long entertained, as to the position in which traces of Franklin would be found, in order that your Lordships may judge whether the further observations, which I feel it my duty to make upon the subject, are not entitled to more consideration than my former suggestions have received at the hands of Her Majesty's Government.

There is an important question now before your Lordships. Has everything, in the power of the English Government, been done to obtain evidence of the death of The Franklin Expedition? I unhesitatingly answer in the negative.

From the statements of the Esquimaux seen by Dr. Rae, taken in connection with the evidence procured by the last searching party, there seems little doubt that a considerable number of white men died at or near Point Ogle, on the western coast of the embouchure of Great Fish River, and that a smaller party, consisting of an officer and four men, died on Montreal Island,—a spot about half a day's journey to the South of Point Ogle. This last party had a boat with them, which was subsequently sawn up by the Esquimaux, who left a quantity of chips, on one of which was found the word "Terror." A number of articles of common use, and even of luxury, belonging to the expedition, have been purchased from the Esquimaux, and brought to England, but the inquiries of the last searching party could find no trace of any papers, records, or other written documents!

Such, then, are the simple facts before us, and, without entering upon the vexed question as to the manner in which our unfortunate countrymen met their death, whether by starvation, or by the hands of the Esquimaux, the chief point for inquiry appears to be;—For what purpose did an officer and four men visit Montreal Island? As the iron coast of an inhospitable little Island is the last place to which an Arctic traveller would resort for provisions, it is evident that the visit must be assigned to some other cause, and this point, which seems at present to be a mystery, it is, I think, in my power to elucidate.

On my visit to Montreal Island in 1834,

I constructed a hiding-place, which was known by the name of "King Cache," and which was subsequently visited and opened by Simpson in 1839, in the same manner as the Cache made by Parry on Melville Island, called "Parry Sandstone," was opened by McClure in 1852. *The existence of my Cache was known to Franklin,* and it is my firm belief that he, or the leading survivor of the Expedition, crossed over from Point Ogle for the purpose of searching this Cache, and of depositing there a record of his visit, and that he and his boat's crew subsequently met their death before they could regain the main land.

By whatever means they perished, I think there can be no doubt that the leader, knowing of the existence of my Cache, and trusting that it would be searched ere long by friends from home, would strain every nerve, before he ceased to live, to deposit in this place of safety, not only the memorial of his visit, which he crossed from the mainland for the purpose of placing there, but also the history, which he would most unquestionably have carried with him, of the endurance and the sufferings of that devoted band, and of the heroic constancy with which the officers had sustained the flagging courage of their men, in the speedy hope of receiving that succour which, by a horrible fatality, had been directed to every point of the Polar Seas, except the precise spot on which they then stood. And the fact that no papers were found in the hands of the Esquimaux, is in itself a strong presumption that the records of the Expedition had been deposited in a place of safety before the death of our hapless countrymen.

In the official report of the leader of the last searching party, my Cache is not mentioned, and, as he would scarcely have omitted to search it, or have forgotten to refer to it in his report, if he had been aware of its existence, I cannot but conclude that, by some further and unexplained misfortune, he started on his journey without being aware that Montreal Island contained any particular spot in which there would unquestionably be found some traces of the missing Expedition.

From these facts, I can only draw the deduction that, in all human probability, a history of The Franklin Expedition still lies buried in my Cache, beneath the rocky shore of Montreal Island, and that it is within the bounds of possibility that this record may be recovered, and that the discoveries of the ill-fated Expedition may yet be published for the advancement of science, and the narrative of their probably unexampled sufferings be made known to the world.

Under these circumstances, I feel assured that the people of England will not consent that the search for the missing Expedition shall rest in its present position. More than two millions sterling has already been squandered in expeditions, which have brought home no tidings of the lost navigators, beyond a few silver forks and other relics, and an apocryphal story, interpreted from the vague signs of the Esquimaux, too revolting in its details to be worthy of implicit belief.

A further Land Journey down Great Fish River may be performed at a cost of about £.1000, and this Journey, if your Lordships will give me the command of a party, I offer, for *the fifth time*, to undertake, in the confident hope that I may yet, at the eleventh hour, be the means of recovering a record of the Expedition, the recital of whose sufferings will otherwise be buried in everlasting oblivion.

I have the honour to be, my Lords, &c.,

17, Savile Row, 23 Jan. '56. RICHARD KING.

SIR, Admiralty, 28th Jan. 1856.

Having laid before my Lords Commissioners of the Admiralty your letter of the 21st instant, volunteering your services to command an Expedition by Land down the Great Fish River to Montreal Island, to search for traces of the fate of the late Sir John Franklin and Party, I am commanded by their Lordships to acquaint you that they do not think it advisable to undertake such an Expedition.

I am, &c.,

DR. KING, M.D. THOS PHINN.

LONDON:
PRINTED BY T. BRETTELL, RUPERT STREET, HAYMARKET.

For EU product safety concerns, contact us at Calle de José Abascal, 56–1°,
28003 Madrid, Spain or eugpsr@cambridge.org.

www.ingramcontent.com/pod-product-compliance
Ingram Content Group UK Ltd.
Pitfield, Milton Keynes, MK11 3LW, UK
UKHW010343140625
459647UK00010B/797

* 9 7 8 1 1 0 8 0 7 1 6 4 2 *